Bill ~

From all of us in Bulk Power Trading who are fortunate to have worked with you. We hope you return often, if only in spirit, as you reminisce about your memories of Chattanooga.

Larry Taylor

CHATTANOOGA
River City Renaissance

CHATTANOOGA
River City Renaissance

By June Scobee Rodgers

✳

Profiles in Excellence by Jack Makuch

✳

Captions by Pam Sohn

✳

Art Direction by Enrique Espinosa

✳

Sponsored by the Chattanooga
Area Chamber of Commerce

**URBAN
TAPESTRY
SERIES**

TOWERY
PUBLISHING, INC.

LIBRARY OF CONGRESS CATALOGING-IN-PUBLICATION DATA

Rodgers, June Scobee.
   Chattanooga : river city renaissance / by June Scobee Rodgers ;
Profiles in excellence by Jack Makuch ; captions by Pam Sohn ; art
direction by Enrique Espinosa.
     p. cm. — (Urban tapestry series)
   "Sponsored by the Chattanooga Area Chamber of Commerce."
   ISBN 1-881096-59-9 (alk. paper)
   1. Chattanooga (Tenn.)—Civilization. 2. Chattanooga (Tenn.)-
-Pictorial works. 3. Chattanooga (Tenn.)—Economic conditions.
4. Business enterprises—Tennessee—Chattanooga.   I. Makuch, Jack,
1951- . II. Title. III. Title: River city renaissance.
IV. Series
F444.C45R63   1998
976.8'82—dc21   98-37335

TOWERY PUBLISHING, INC.
The Towery Building, 1835 UNION AVENUE, MEMPHIS, TN 38104

PUBLISHER: J. Robert Towery
EXECUTIVE PUBLISHER: Jenny McDowell
ASSOCIATE PUBLISHER: Michael C. James
NATIONAL SALES MANAGER: Stephen Hung
MARKETING DIRECTOR: Carol Culpepper
PROJECT DIRECTORS: Robert Philips, Anne Walker

EXECUTIVE EDITOR: David B. Dawson
MANAGING EDITOR: Lynn Conlee
SENIOR EDITOR: Carlisle Hacker
EDITOR/PROJECT MANAGER: Brian Johnston
EDITORS: Mary Jane Adams, Lori Bond, Jana Files,
        John Floyd, Barry Willis
ASSISTANT EDITOR: Rebecca Green
EDITORIAL ASSISTANT: Sunni Thompson
EDITORIAL CONTRIBUTOR: Karen L. Nystrom

CREATIVE DIRECTOR: Brian Groppe
PHOTOGRAPHY EDITOR: Jonathan Postal
PHOTOGRAPHIC CONSULTANT: Billy Weeks
PROFILE DESIGNERS: Laurie Beck, Kelley Pratt, Ann Ward
DIGITAL COLOR SUPERVISOR: Darin Ipema
DIGITAL COLOR TECHNICIANS: John Brantley, Eric Friedl, Brent Salazar
PRODUCTION RESOURCES MANAGER: Dave Dunlap Jr.
PRODUCTION ASSISTANT: Robin McGehee
PRINT COORDINATOR: Tonda Thomas

© TROY E. MOORE SR.

Contents

L OVE IS IN THE AIR, AND IN DOWNTOWN CHATTANOOGA, IT'S MORE THAN ROMANCE, IT'S A RENaissance. Chattanooga is humming with renewal. And if you listen, you can hear it all around. Since opening the Tennessee Aquarium and Riverwalk in 1992, Chattanooga has reinvented its downtown area a block at a time. You can hear the progressive tempo of the whole city in the rhythm of footsteps, in the hum of CARTA's electric shuttle buses, in the splish splash of children playing in the water parks on the city plaza. You can hear the new song in the shrill screams and muffled giggles of children in their own Creative Discovery Museum, or in the thunderous applause of the spectators at the University of Tennessee, Chattanooga's new Finley Stadium.

On a more mercantile note—and perhaps a louder one—you can hear the gears and wheels of Chattanooga's renewal being turned in the sounds of construction vehicles, hammers, cement mixers, and cranes, all of them rebuilding and reenergizing downtown.

In addition to hearing the changes, you can *see* them throughout the area. For a spectacular sight, catch the view from atop the Republic Centre building. There, you can see how Chattanooga's skyline tells the story of the city, blessed as it is with old and new buildings alike, and animated by more than 60 new restaurants, shops, hotels, and theaters. From the Chattanooga Choo-Choo Holiday Inn to the lofty sail-like peaks of the Tennessee Aquarium; from stately old homes to newly constructed neighborhoods; from the new Bijou Theater to the state-of-the-art IMAX; from the brick street sculptures all over downtown to the antique Fischer-Evans clock: It's all visible from here atop the Republic Centre, where you can see the renaissance unfolding in every direction.

The riverfront captures your attention immediately with its graceful Southern front-porch welcome to the city—the place where downtown meets the Tennessee River, teeming with ageless activity. Dads and kids with fishing poles; families on sailboats and jet skis; college students in canoes; the *Southern Belle* riverboat's timeless charm; and the daily tugs and barges making their way up the river—all are hallmarks of the new riverfront, the renovated area where John Ross, a Cherokee Indian, ran his ferry service nearly two centuries ago and where the city itself was launched.

The centerpiece of the riverfront is the majestic Tennessee Aquarium, the largest freshwater aquarium in the world. Not unlike a great wall of mountains, the soaring structure reverently tells the story of the river in a spectacular 60-foot "canyon" that is home to some 9,000 swimming, flying, and crawling animals living in two "forests." The aquarium and the surrounding plaza serve as the linchpin in Chattanooga's rebirth, thanks to our citizens' visionary process, old-fashioned entrepreneurship, informed philanthropy, and the guidance and support of our city's government, all of which came together to make the riverfront a focal point for community activity and development.

The aquarium traces the formation of the river in an innovative and interactive display: Moving stairs take visitors high into the mountain coves of an Appalachian forest, where river otters play and birds fly overhead and the web of life spreads all around. Eventually, the stairs come to the very source of the river, where moisture beads up on leaves and falls in droplets to the earth. There, around green moss-covered rocks, the water coalesces and glides down a wet path, tugged by gravity to trickle into streams, cascade over cliffs, and join other streams before finally reaching its ultimate destination— the mighty Tennessee. ☛

BY
JUNE
SCOBEE
RODGERS

S TANDING IN TESTAMENT TO LOCAL historic preservation efforts, the Dome Building is a prime example of Chattanooga's lovely turn-of-the-century architecture (OPPOSITE).

© DOUG BARNETTE

Chattanooga

THE PLAZA THAT SURROUNDS THE AQUARIUM CONTAINS A HISTORY LESSON IN THE FORM OF A series of landscaped bands that interweave public art and native plants to tell the story of our community and its relationship with the Tennessee River. These bands trace area history from the time of its earliest inhabitants through several significant historic periods, including the history of Native Americans, Chattanooga's railroad heritage, the Civil War, the world's first Coca-Cola bottling operation, and legendary blues singer Bessie Smith. I love to watch barefoot children on steamy hot days wade into the spraying fountains or the flowing stream that winds through the middle of the plaza. Their smiles somehow speak volumes about the aquarium, the riverfront it graces, and the big river that flows silently nearby.

The IMAX Theater occupies the western section of the site. From all directions, the IMAX center's most visible feature is the glazed cylinder tower, whose base contains the theater's box office. High above, the tower opens like a child's hand reaching to the sky.

Adding a piece of zany architecture to Chattanooga's skyline, the Creative Discovery Museum welcomes kids of all ages to explore hands-on exhibits relating to art, music, and dinosaurs. The three-story, interactive tower, topped by its landmark weather vane, provides plenty for children and their parents to explore together in a museum created to appeal to the far reaches of the imagination.

If you're looking at the city from atop the Republic Centre, just beyond the Provident Insurance buildings you will see, on tall limestone cliffs, an area informally known as the downtown arts district. Here you will find the Hunter Museum of American Art, a recently renovated mansion that houses one of the largest and finest collections of American art in the Southeast. Across the street, the Houston

Museum of Decorative Arts displays the antique glass, china, and furniture collection of Anna Safley Houston in the warmth and charm of a turn-of-the-century home. Having married at least nine times, the wonderfully eccentric woman—known as "Crazy Annie"—amassed her collection despite a life of modest means.

Adjacent to the museums is a creative haven created by the Portera family. This block, the Bluff View Art District, is filled with museums, restaurants, courtyard gardens, galleries, terrace cafés, meeting rooms, and elegant overnight accommodations with outstanding views of the river. Rounding out the Bluff View Art District is the River Gallery Sculpture Garden, where families enjoy art and nature on the beautifully landscaped grounds.

Across Veterans Bridge, Hixson Pike reaches into the Riverview business district. On the corner, the Plum Nelly greets shoppers with an artistic display of craft items and an intriguing story about how it got its whimsical name: A tradition began more than 50 years ago on the back side of Lookout Mountain at an outdoor clothesline art show that attracted thousands of art lovers. A visitor traveling from out of town said the art show was "plum" out of Tennessee, and "nelly" out of Georgia. While the shows are no longer held, their spirit has been preserved by the Plum Nelly Shop.

Looking off to the east (from the perch atop the Republic Centre), you can see the sign for the grand old Tivoli Theatre. This sign evokes different memories for different people. When I see it, I think of a *Nutcracker* mouse king, grand concerts under the direction of Bob Bernhardt, classic operas, and children's recitals. ☞

WITH ITS CLEVER, SAIL-LIKE DESIGN, the Tennessee Aquarium appears to float along Chattanooga's skyline as progress continues to alter the landscape along the gentle Tennessee River (OPPOSITE). Located next door, the IMAX Theater launches its own architectural fireworks into the sunset (ABOVE).

As a matter of fact, Chattanooga's vibrant and evolving glow is visible in every direction (PAGES 10 AND 11).

WE CHATTANOOGANS LIKE TO BOAST ABOUT OUR CITY. WE BRAG ABOUT THE AQUARIUM. Or Hamilton Place, Tennessee's largest shopping mall. Or Chickamauga/Chattanooga National Military Park, the nation's first and largest such park. Or Tom Thumb's Miniature Golf, one of the first in the country, which was located on Lookout Mountain. ✳ We also have the world's steepest passenger railway, the Lookout Mountain Incline Railway. We talk about our square hamburgers (Krystal), about our being the birthplace of bottled Coca-Cola, and about the marshmallow-and-graham-cracker Moon Pie—one of the staples of Southern haute cuisine—that was invented here.

We like to brag about the Riverbend Festival, an event that captures the spirit of community and the joy of success. During Riverbend, we gather to give summertime a big, warm welcome with special events, lots of food, and the best in live music from national recording artists and rising stars. The festival has the biggest fireworks show of the year capping off a week and a half of riverfront fun. On one of the nights of the festival, the Bessie Smith Strut occurs on M.L. King Boulevard, featuring the best blues bands anywhere, along with a cast of thousands of enthusiastic fans.

In fact, it was a series of weekly downtown concerts in the early 1980s—called Five Nights in Chattanooga—that helped set the stage not only for the explosion of music in Chattanooga, but for bringing together a diverse audience to enjoy the city's commonly shared pleasures. Downtown concerts are still enjoyed as the Nightfall Concert Series in Miller Plaza draws crowds each Friday night during the summer.

Much as we like to brag and celebrate ourselves, though, we haven't been the only ones noticing something special about our city. In recent years, the accolades have been numerous and on target.

Family Fun magazine featured Chattanooga as one of the 10 best family-friendly vacation cities in the United States.

U.S. News & World Report named Chattanooga one of six "smart cities" in the world.

Walking magazine named Chattanooga as one of the 16 most "walkable" communities in the country.

And the alternative *Utne Reader* has named our city one of the Ten Most Enlightened Towns in America.

Rather than trying to present too much of a good thing, it's worth noting that Chattanooga's story wasn't always so bright, and there seemed, at times, to be precious little to brag about. The city has met adversity and overcome difficulty so many times throughout its history that it could easily be dubbed Survival City. We've endured, and recovered, from plenty: war (the Civil War battles of Chickamauga, Lookout Mountain, and Missionary Ridge), pestilence (cholera and yellow fever), and floods (a devastating one in 1867 nearly wiped out the city). ☛

AT THE HUNTER MUSEUM OF American Art, even the fence is a masterpiece (OPPOSITE). Perched atop the bluffs overlooking the Tennessee River, the museum holds one of the premier collections of American art in the Southeast. The facility's sculpture garden is so popular that it has influenced outdoor art across the city, including this piece near the Tennessee Valley Authority's downtown complex (BELOW).

© BUD LEE

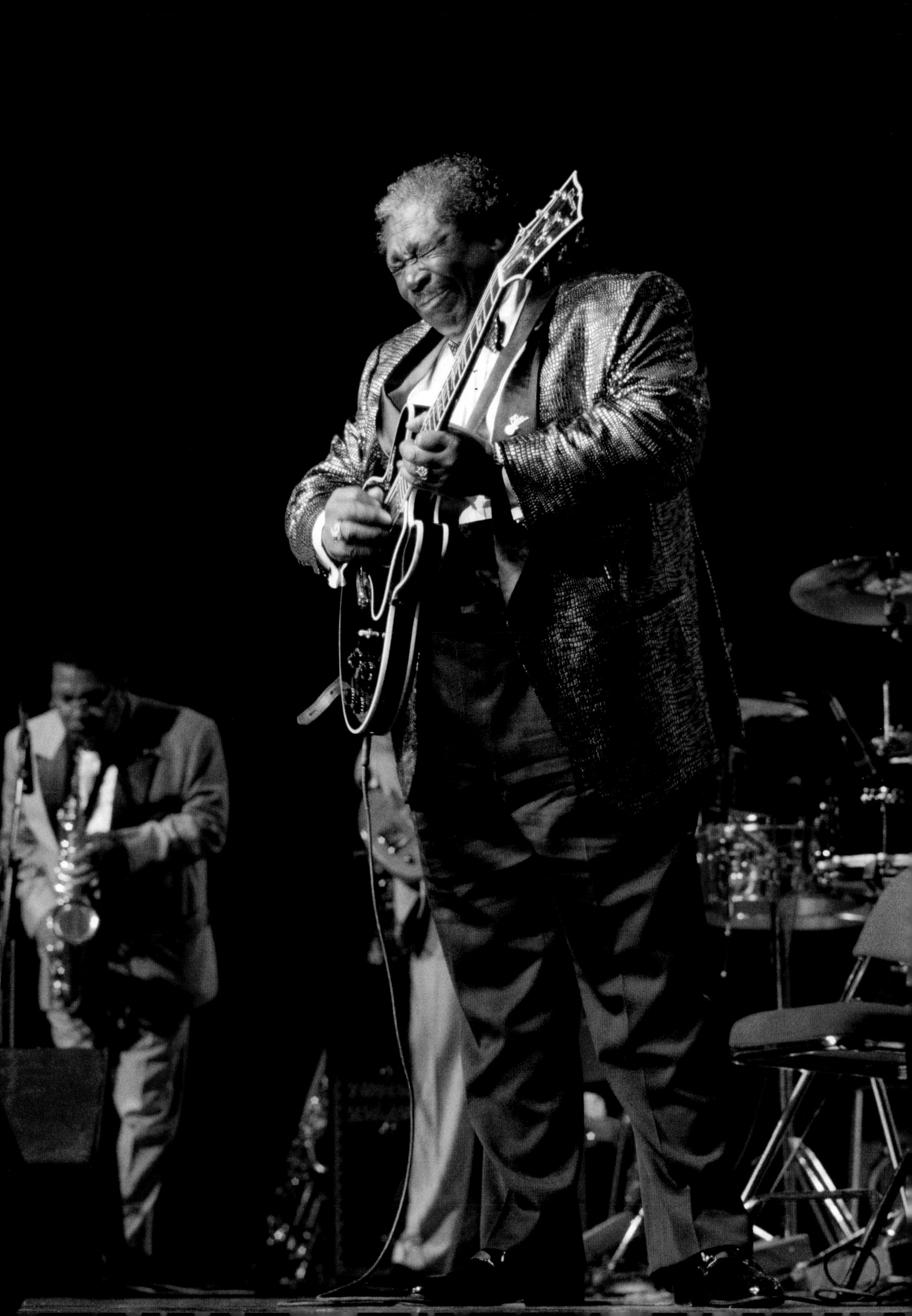

WHETHER IT'S GUITAR GREAT B.B. King electrifying local audiences (PAGE 15) or a shrine to blues legend Bessie Smith (PAGE 14), music continues to play an important role in Chattanooga life.

Doing its part to keep the era of steam passenger trains alive, the Tennessee Valley Railroad Museum offers 6.5-mile excursions on a classic, restored steam locomotive.

Through it all, Chattanooga has managed to grow and thrive. The city began with John Ross' ferry landing in the 1820s. It became a railroad center (the Chattanooga Choo-Choo isn't just hype) and, in time, a center for industry, manufacturing, services, the arts, and tourism. From the parade of progress begun in the early 20th century—which lit up the town with electric lights—to the first bottling of a popular Atlanta fountain beverage, Coca-Cola, by some men who were reputedly looking for a handy way to take their favorite soft drink to the ballpark, to the modern era of textiles, synthetics, technology, and telecommunications, Chattanooga has weathered its storms and emerged from its difficulties as one of the South's most vibrant cities. The Tennessee Valley Authority is headquartered in Chattanooga, and while most people think of TVA as a provider of electricity (which it certainly *is*), this entity is also a powerful force in developing the region and keeping it on the vanguard of progress.

Although we had abandoned the riverfront to the factories and foundries sometime in the 1960s—a common urban predicament—it was these manufacturing firms that helped provide jobs and kept the city from going under. Today, Chattanooga remains a manufacturing center, and is home to, among others, Komatsu American International Company, which is currently undergoing an expansion at its heavy machinery manufacturing plant that was established here in the mid-1980s.

Much of the credit for the city's renaissance goes to a series of public/private initiatives spearheaded by civic and business leaders, government officials, and private citizens anxious to see Chattanooga thrive. Through such 1980s efforts as Vision 2000 (a goal-setting program involving the entire community), Chattanooga Venture (a task-oriented program of changes), and a number of other important civic and entrepreneurial efforts, the renaissance began to take shape. Similar programs have lately been inaugurated under the banner of Sustainable Development, as those doing the planning seek ways to ensure that future generations will enjoy a better environment, a better economy, and a better city. With an innovative police chief helping to implement community policing programs, as well as a spirit of helping those who need to be helped (Chattanooga is a perennial leader in donations to private charitable organizations), there's a feeling in the air that we are, indeed, masters of our destiny. Helping to demonstrate this are programs such as Chattanooga Neighborhood Enterprise, a public/private partnership that has won national acclaim for its efforts to provide affordable housing for all who are determined to own or improve their homes and neighborhoods. ☛

IT WAS CHATTANOOGA'S STATUS AS a rail and river hub that made it such a prize in the Civil War. Even today, locals gather for authentic re-enactments of the numerous battles that took place across the East Tennessee landscape.

AFTER EARLY SUCCESS IN THE ROSS' LANDING DISTRICT SURROUNDING THE TENNESSEE AQUARIUM, Chattanooga's urban redevelopment programs have lately been expanding to a more ambitious second phase in the industrial Southside of downtown. We are transforming abandoned factories and foundries, as well as warehouses and weedy vacant lots, into a residential and commercial development to complement the urban character of the neighborhood. On tap are an expanded convention center with new conferencing and training facilities, new housing like that created with the renovation of the old Grand Hotel, and a host of great new restaurants to complement the ones that we've come to love downtown. Already, UTC's Finley Stadium, cradled in colors of blue and gold, welcomes throngs of spectators to the newly refurbished Southside. Across the street from the stadium, we've cleaned up the old Ross-Mehan Foundry building that was abandoned and covered over with trumpet vines. Today, the structure has a new life as an open-air pavilion for concerts in the summer and ice-skating in the winter.

The Tennessee World Trade Center, headquartered on the Southside, helps companies compete in the global economy. And plans for a new ecoindustrial park have drawn attention from government and academic institutions for their efforts to maintain a healthy balance between the ecology and the economy.

Strategically located between research and development communities, Chattanooga is quickly becoming a regional center for technological research and manufacturing. The East Tennessee Technology Corridor has been formed to aid and foster the dozens of economic initiatives that have come together to help spawn high-tech investment in cutting-edge technologies.

Yet cutting-edge, futuristic development is by no means the sole focus of Chattanooga's renaissance. We aim to preserve and enhance the best from our past, as well. The historic Walnut Street Bridge is a perfect example of the ways in which community efforts have helped create a tangible link between past and future. Rather than demolish the bridge—as was planned—we fully restored it as the world's longest pedestrian bridge, with the names of donors inscribed on small brass plates on the planks that form the bridge. ☛

GENTLE FOGS LEND AN AIR OF NOStalgia to the scenic Tennessee River as it traverses Chattanooga.

THE WALNUT STREET BRIDGE IS BUT ONE EMBLEM OF THE WAYS IN WHICH THE CITY TREASURES ITS heritage and seeks to retain the best of the past. The Dome Building, a richly ornamented Italian Renaissance structure, was originally built by Adolph Ochs to house the offices of the *Chattanooga Times*. (A less auspicious downtown business, Buehler Market, also has a tie to the city's newspaper history: The market is a direct descendant of the old Home Stores groceries, once owned by Roy McDonald, who was also owner of the *Chattanooga Free Press*. The paper—which really was free—was founded in 1936 as an advertising vehicle for McDonald's Home Stores.) Other prominent downtown structures from yesteryear include the beautifully ornamented James and Maclellan buildings.

Flags wave against the white stone walls of the Federal Building, reminding all who pass of our American heritage. Yet for each of us, that heritage has a different meaning. Chattanooga is home to several institutions that reflect the diversity that is protected and honored here. Just beyond the Federal Building, for instance, is Heritage Hall on M.L. King Boulevard. Home to the Chattanooga African-American History Museum, it also contains Bessie Smith Hall, which honors the hometown legend who became the Empress of the Blues.

The University of Tennessee at Chattanooga's Fletcher Hall has been renovated, retaining its old-world charm on the exterior while offering College of Business students a high-tech haven inside. Peeking out across the campus and trees are rooftops of the Fort Wood historic neighborhood. Houses in the Queen Anne, Victorian, and classical revival styles are some of the favorites that bring new families to join longtime residents to create a viable inner-city residential section. ☛

COCA-COLA HAS A SPECIAL PLACE IN the hearts—and tastebuds—of Chattanoogans. While the drink itself originated in Atlanta, the world's first Coca-Cola bottling plant opened here in 1899. Another nationally known local icon, Rock City Gardens once inspired the painting of as many as 900 barns bearing the slogan See Rock City.

B ARBECUE FOR BREAKFAST, LUNCH— *and* dinner? Not necessarily. From cozy cafés to fine dining establishments, the Chattanooga area has more than 1,100 restaurants guaranteed to suit every taste and mood.

Of course, some people prefer the catch of the day from the Tennessee River (PAGES 26 AND 27), where the views are inspiring in any light.

A truck filled with Little Debbie Snack Cakes traveling up Eighth Street reminds me that the interstate that cuts through the mountain ridge leads to Ooltewah's covered bridges, cozy neighborhoods, and dairy farms. Located nearby is the McKee Foods Corporation, cofounded by O.D. and Ruth McKee in Collegedale, where they created the Little Debbie line of pastries and cookies, named after their granddaughter. The business began with Mr. McKee's selling cakes from the backseat of his car, a 1928 Whippet.

And as for the city's heritage, we can't forget the venerable Choo-Choo hotel, once part of the legendary rail station, and now a vacation complex where families can sleep in converted train cars and children can climb aboard a bright red-and-green vintage locomotive. I love the complex best during the winter holidays when carolers sing, and the massive domed reception area and lobby become a nostalgic setting for a Victorian winter wonderland, a reminder of bygone days when it was a thriving railroad terminal.

Further to the south is Lookout Mountain. From a distance, it often seems mystical, sometimes jutting out like a prow on a ship in the fog. No wonder Frieda and Garnet Carter were inspired years ago to create the fairyland center at Rock City Gardens, a wonderful family experience that combines spectacular natural scenery and rock formations with the enchantment of a child's imagination. Garnet also planned the Fairyland (pronounced "fairylun" by locals) community that carries the theme over into neighborhoods with street names like Red Riding Hood, Peter Pan, and Cinderella. Beautiful homes and churches in natural settings adorn the rolling hills. It's also home to flight schools and Covenant College, known fondly by many as the castle in the sky. It's a people-friendly place where community spirit soars.

And just below the mountain, there's no place more beautiful in the spring than Reflection Riding, a 300-acre nature preserve—established in 1956—where thousands of trees, shrubs, and wildflowers bloom and grace numerous walking trails. For those who don't want to leave their cars, there are several miles of automobile routes to take through the gardens. ☛

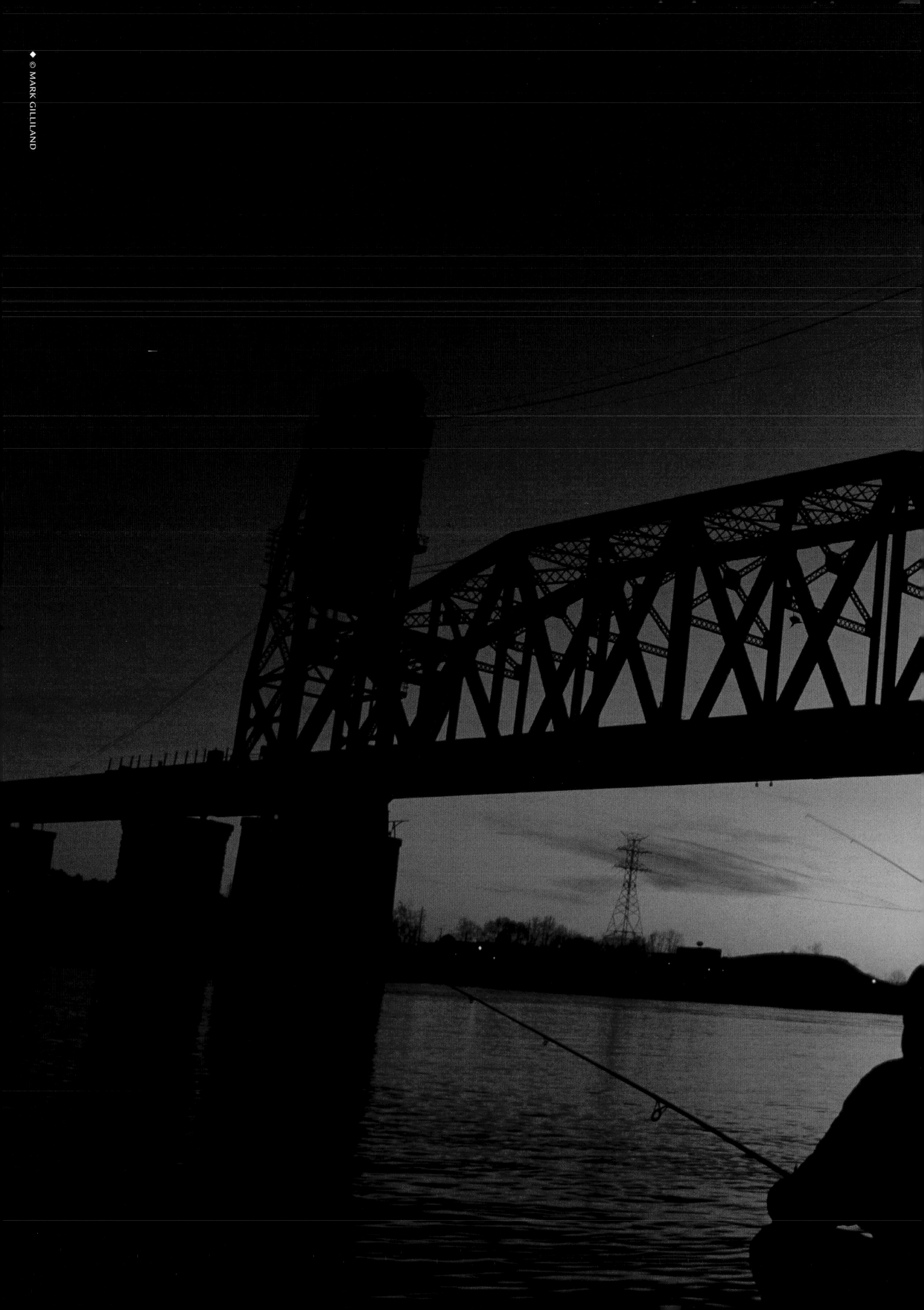

© MARK GILLILAND

Lookout Mountain, the Southside, downtown—all are good areas to see both the heritage and the resurgence of Chattanooga. But they are by no means the only places to witness the area's renaissance. There are plans for a new town square for the Eastgate area. West of downtown, the First Baptist steeple stands tall near Fourth Street where Highway 27 welcomes travelers to the city and bids them good-bye—south toward Lookout or north over the Olgiati Bridge toward Red Bank and Soddy-Daisy. The northern route features the Scenic Highway 127 cutoff to Signal Mountain, the city on Walden's Ridge.

Also on that route, the road climbs up a steep winding path into a cavernous forest of kudzu vines, then corners up and around the famous round "space house" (a spaceship-looking residence that has become something of a local landmark) till it reaches the top. At this summit, travelers are welcomed by a plaque honoring Signal Mountain's founding father, Charles "Charlie" James, the businessman who promoted the development of the town. James led the drive to incorporate so that ordinances could be passed and fences could be built in an attempt to keep the roaming cattle from eating the grass on the private lawns.

Village stores provide just about everything Signal Mountain's citizens (and I am one of them) require, running short of milk and bread only when there's a threat of snow or ice storms that make traveling down the "W" (the rock-lined road that winds up to the town) a treacherous ordeal. (The W once led to a place named Summertown, so-called because it was the ideal location to escape the summer heat of the valley below.)

There's a spirit of community on the mountain—neighbors who bond, people who speak of its history with reverence. I know this from the long conversations I have with other customers waiting in line at the Bread Basket Bakery, especially during the holidays. Those of us who live here are truly proud of how all the citizens on Walden's Ridge came together to build a magnificent children's playground in an old pumpkin patch. ☛

Everyday life on Chattanooga streets exudes community, typified by downtown police on bicycle patrol or the friendly murmurs of conversation as locals take a minute to catch up.

The city also has its share of colorful sights: A Tennessee Aquarium worker mingles with some exotic underwater creatures (PAGE 30), and, at 145 feet, Ruby Falls never fails to dazzle its constant stream of visitors (PAGE 31).

BUT GRAND VISTAS, TIME-HONORED DELIGHTS, AND PUMPKIN PATCHES ARE NOT ALL WE LOVE ABOUT Chattanooga. We have our sports—an abundance of tennis courts, parks, softball diamonds, swimming pools, and golf courses prove it. And we have Engle Stadium, home of the Class AA minor-league Lookouts, as well as the legendary softball Stadium of a Thousand Dreams at Warner Park. Side roads and trails lead to hundreds of nooks and crannies along lakes, coves, and creeks. Outstanding recreational opportunities abound, such as nature preserves, greenways, bike paths, hang-gliding ramps, motocross tracks, and rivers to fish, canoe, and white-water rafting.

We have four glorious seasons in which to enjoy all of our outdoor activities. Chattanooga's beauty is ever changing, with new wonders and delights appearing every season. I love to see sleepy daffodils peeking out from a blanket of snow in late winter, only to feel, within days, the blustery March winds blowing away the gray curtain of winter. Spring welcomes gardens that explode with brilliant color, calling for the celebrations marked by numerous area wildflower festivals. Summer brings lush greenery to the hillsides and deep cool shade to the woods, as well as hot sunshine to the pools and swimming holes that dot the area. October glows with gold-washed afternoons meant for relaxing under a canopy of yellow-leafed branches, while the surrounding mountains blaze with fiery fall color. Then, December delivers the splendor of a winter moon so big that its reflection makes the snow-tipped mountaintops shine as bright as the winter lights of downtown. And ice crystals form at the edge of ponds and lakes up in the mountains; waterfalls freeze solid; midday sunbeams turn the icy woods into a glittering wonderland.

Even with all of this and more—the grand rebuilding campaigns and the small delights provided by the changing of the seasons—many still find it remarkable that the city's rebirth has been so thorough, so rapid, and so rich. The will of Chattanoogans to reclaim their neglected waterfront and to rebuild all corners of their city has proved to be as much of a surprise as one of the sudden snowstorms we enjoy each winter.

And yet, our renaissance continues to attract news stories from other cities, where headlines tell the tale for us: "The Cinderella Story." "Turnaround City." "Clean and Green." "A Lesson in Rebirth."

But those who know Chattanooga's history and her people know that this is a city that has many facets and many faces. Chattanooga is both a journey and a destination. It's a city that's moving constantly into the future—a community on a wide river whose winding path through green mountains beckons us, always, toward home. ❧

WINDOWS OF OPPORTUNITY: The view is always great in Chattanooga, where a reverence for the past and an eye toward the future characterize this city on the go.

© DAVID M. GRANT

OPENED IN 1895, THE INCLINE RAILway lays claim to being America's Most Amazing Mile. Moving up and down Lookout Mountain at almost a 73-degree angle near its highest point, the train is also the steepest passenger railway in the world. The trolley-style cars deposit riders within walking distance of Point Park, the Civil War site of the Battle above the Clouds.

CHATTANOOGA

WHETHER A ROCK JOCK OR A WIN-dow doc, adventurists of all kinds find the heights of Chattanooga's natural and man-made sites challenging and often thrilling.

THE AREA'S UNIQUE LUSHNESS and beauty beckon outdoor enthusiasts to such natural treasures as Audubon Acres. Located in East Brainerd, the 128-acre wooded site features some 10 miles of hiking trails, as well as an old-fashioned, 50-year-old swinging bridge across South Chickamauga Creek (OPPOSITE). Visitors to the 16,000-acre South Cumberland State Park and Natural Area, located west of the city in Monteagle, can plant their feet atop the Stone Door overlook for a visual taste of southeast Tennessee's spectacular autumn foliage (ABOVE).

Visitors have traveled from all over the country to Rock City Gardens (PAGES 40-43). The classic American attraction has it all—plenty of trails; Lover's Leap, with a spectacular view of seven states; Fat Man's Squeeze; and Mushroom Rock. For the children, Fairyland Caverns and Mother Goose Village round out Rock City's family-pleasing offerings.

The mountains, valleys, and thermal air currents of Chattanooga's terrain have prompted some to call the area the hang gliding capital of the world. Wanna-be gliders can seek a bird's-eye view of the landscape by taking lessons from atop Lookout Mountain and other peaks.

THE WOODS AND MOUNTAINS THAT enclose Chattanooga provide the ideal setting for such community assets as the Chattanooga Nature Center. Typical of its many contributions to the animal kingdom, the center releases a once-injured, red-tailed hawk back into the wild (OPPOSITE). Area bird-watchers can also spot a variety of other winged wonders, like the professorial great horned owl (LEFT) or the barn owl, with its distinctive heart-shaped face (RIGHT).

CHATTANOOGA IS ONE OF THE FEW cities in the country that still celebrate Armed Forces Day with an annual parade. The festivities also include a show at the Chattanooga Metropolitan Airport's Lovell Field, where military aircraft like this C5B Galaxy cargo jet are on public display (ABOVE AND OPPOSITE).

At the National Cemetery, World War I veteran George Zimmerman shows his patriotism during Memorial Day ceremonies (PAGES 50 AND 51). Established in December 1863, the cemetery is the final resting place for more than 12,000 Union soldiers who lost their lives on the many Civil War battle sites in the area. The most notable interments are those of the famed Andrews Raiders, seven of whom were the first-ever recipients of the Congressional Medal of Honor.

OPENED IN 1890, THE 8,200-ACRE Chickamauga and Chattanooga National Military Park in northern Georgia was the first of its kind in the nation. Monuments mark the spots where troops from all over the country gave their lives in the 1863 battle for control of Chattanooga, a months-long siege that marked a turning point in the Civil War.

CIVIL WAR REENACTMENTS IN THE Chattanooga area are commonplace, due in part to the wealth of battle sites nearby. Union troops face the Confederacy once again in a reenactment of the Battle of Tunnel Hill in northern Georgia (TOP, OPPOSITE TOP). Across the Tennessee state line in northeastern Alabama, the Union color guard (OPPOSITE BOTTOM) stands ready for a modern-day Battle of Bridgeport, as the Confederate infantry awaits the call to arms (BOTTOM).

Formed in 1934, the Highlander Pipes and Drums is a unit of the Shrine's Alhambra Temple and the oldest continuously operating Shrine pipe band in North America. The colorful group, which became an independent unit of the temple in 1940, averages 20 to 30 performances annually.

IN ADDITION TO ITS SCOTTISH IN-fluences, Chattanooga is rich in Native American history (PAGES 58 AND 59). The annual, intertribal Raccoon Mountain Indian Festival and Pow Wow features Aztec fire dancers, Cherokee hoop dancers, and traditional foods, such as gator tail and fry bread.

R IDING HORSEBACK MAY CONJURE up images of the pre-automotive past, but equestrian skills are alive and well in Chattanooga. In fact, nearby Chatsworth, Georgia, located some 42 miles southeast of the city, was the site of the Olympic equestrian trials for the 1996 Summer Games in Atlanta.

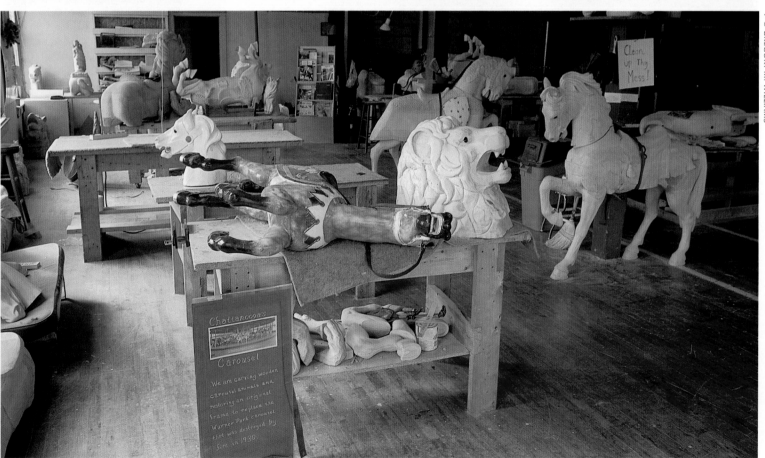

CHATTANOOGA

A HORSE OF A DIFFERENT COLOR is what you'll find at Horsin' Around, a veritable woodworker's dream in St. Elmo. Taking a decidedly hands-on approach, the shop operates the only school in the country that teaches the fine art of carousel carving. This hobby-turned-business will soon hit the big time when owner Bud Ellis and his team of equine-inclined amateurs help create an ornately carved carousel for Chattanooga's new riverfront attraction, Coolidge Park.

610

THE TENNESSEE VALLEY RAILROAD Museum, founded in 1961, celebrates Chattanooga's heyday as a railroad supply center. Home to the largest operating historic railroad in the South, the museum offers an hourly, 6.5 mile ride behind a steam engine through the original 985-foot Missionary Ridge tunnel.

TO AND FROM
DIXIELAND

CHATTANOOGA AND TRAINS. TRAINS and Chattanooga. Pardon me, boy, but didn't Glenn Miller have a famous 1941 song that swept the country and forever linked the city with its choo-choo theme?

THE TENNESSEE RIVER IS AS CENTRAL to Chattanooga now as it was when the city was founded on its banks. The *Southern Bell* (OPPOSITE) offers daily rides past Chattanooga's riverscapes, such as the Hunter Museum, a 1904 mansion that houses one of the country's most prominent American art collections. The *Delta Queen* (ABOVE) makes regular trips through the heart of America's river country, including Chattanooga on its course.

Famous for an abundance of largemouth, smallmouth, and spotted bass, the Tennessee River and its tributaries promise plenty of fabulous fishing (OPPOSITE), not to mention scores of marinas, resorts, and state parks. In addition to its wealth of trout, the nearby Tellico River (ABOVE) is rich in history, including Fort Loudoun, the Sequoyah Birthplace Museum, and the Tellico Blockhouse.

But if you'd rather leave the hooks and bait to others, an exotic "balloon" fish might be more up your alley (PAGES 72 AND 73).

THE INTERNATIONALLY ACCLAIMED Tennessee Aquarium is the largest exhibitor of freshwater ecosystems in the world. Complete with a gorgeous overlook of the Tennessee River, the 130,000-square-foot building holds 400,000 gallons of water and more than 9,000 animals, representing 350 species that swim, fly, and crawl in natural habitats.

Water plays an important role for more than just fish in the Chattanooga area. Whitewater rafting and kayaking on the Ocoee River, home of the 1996 Olympic Whitewater Competition, is open to all levels of rafters for short waves or all-day trips (PAGES 76 AND 77).

CHICKAMAUGA LAKE IS ONE OF NINE waterways formed when the Tennessee Valley Authority began damming the Tennessee River in 1936. The 59-mile lake comes alive each summer with sun-lovers soaking up the rays at one of its most popular swimming and boating areas, Chickamauga Dam.

After a long day at the lake, a retreat to one of the area's friendly, down-home restaurants is just the ticket. And don't forget the ice-cold Coke. Chattanooga was home to the world's first Coca-Cola Bottling Plant (PAGES 82 AND 83).

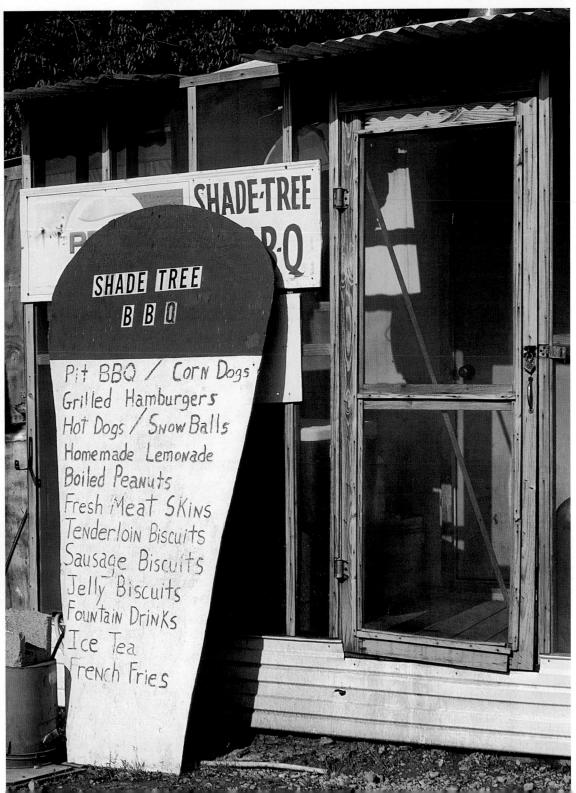

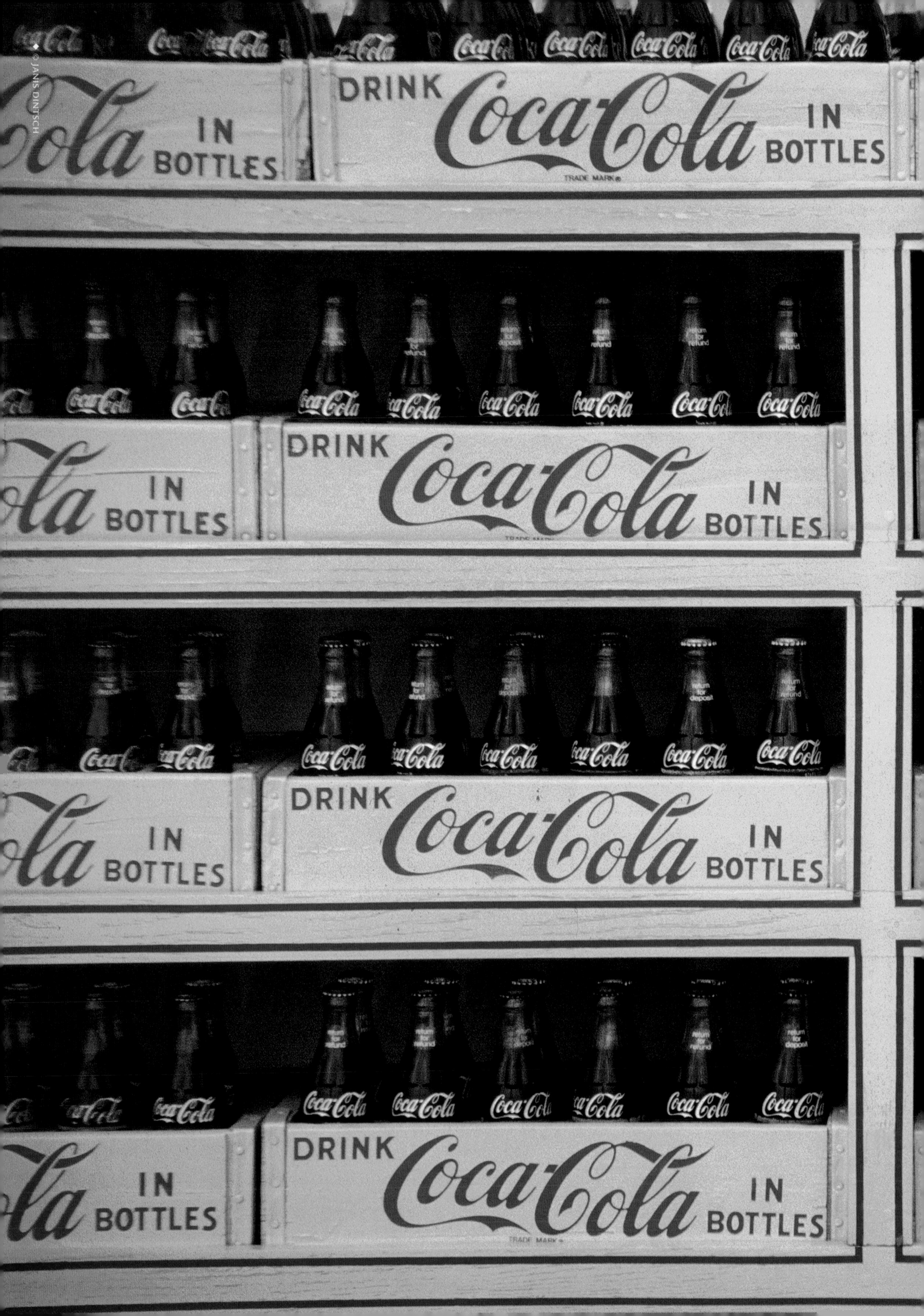

© JANIS DINTSCH

Tastes of the town: The many moods of Chattanooga are reflected in the city's restaurants, which offer a diverse array of dining experiences, including a Mexican eatery with a colorful setting to complement its spicy fare.

For something a little more subdued, many local bars and bistros incorporate mellow lighting and alfresco seating for just the right ambience (PAGES 86 AND 87).

THE BEAT GOES ON FOR BICYCLE cops, who keep a watchful eye on the city as they sail through the night. Innovative community policing has put officers on foot, bicycle, and horseback, as well as in cars. Even more wheels are in motion along Frazier Street in Chattanooga's revitalized Northside neighborhood, a venue for everything from antique shops and specialty stores to health clubs and restaurants.

THEY HAVE THE TOOLS; THEY HAVE the talent: A Chattanooga firefighter battles a downtown blaze with equal amounts of water and courage.

With 19 stations, five ladder trucks, and almost 400 firefighters, the Chattanooga Fire Department protects 125 square miles of homes and businesses.

EQUALLY IMBUED WITH THE AREA'S long-standing work ethic, local welders have much to do as a building boom continues to change the face of the city (PAGES 92 AND 93).

94

THE CHATTANOOGA AREA HAS THE distinction of being home to two of the Tennessee Valley Authority's three nuclear power facilities. Beginning operations in 1981, the Sequoyah Nuclear Plant in nearby Soddy-Daisy (OPPOSITE) today is joined by Watts Bar Nuclear Plant, whose 1996 opening made it the last in the United States to go on-line. Together, the two sites can generate enough electricity to supply 725,000 homes.

CHATTANOOGA

ALL WORK AND NO PLAY MAKES FOR a dull city. For locals whose idea of entertainment is the sound of a six-ball slamming into a side pocket, there are plenty of opportunities for fun and games, including downtown's Chattanooga Billiards Club (OPPOSITE) and the Big River Grill on the waterfront (ABOVE).

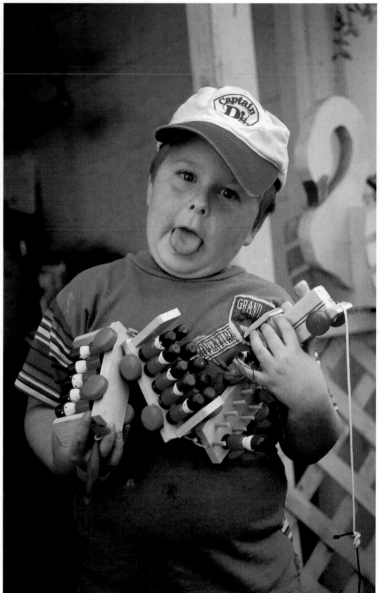

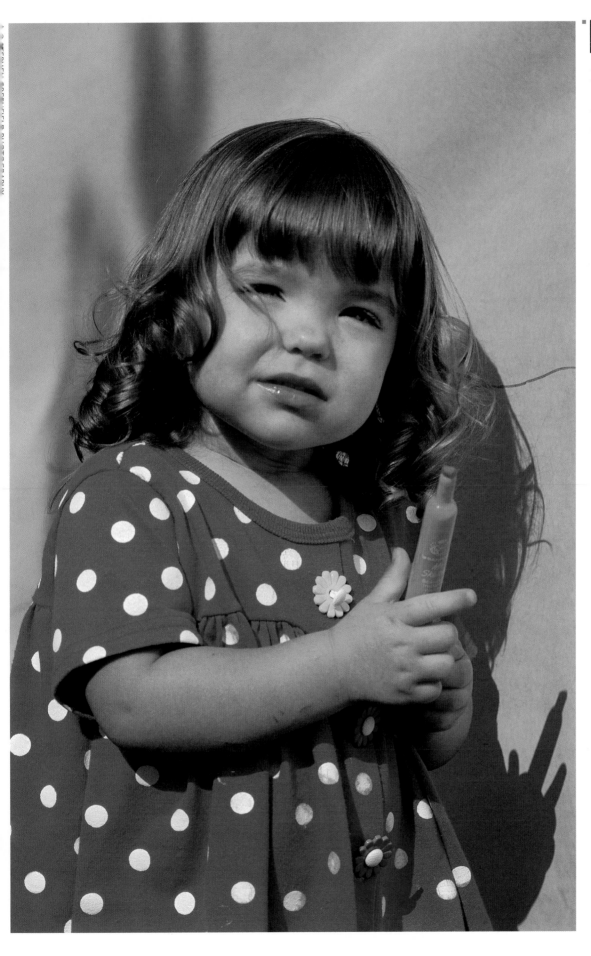

CHATTANOOGA'S ONGOING RENAISsance extends to its younger generation. Give them paintbrushes, toy trains, and magic markers on paperlined walls, and inventive youngsters will make an imaginary city all their own.

Chattanooga's Creative Discovery Museum serves up a plateful of education along with a side dish of fun. Opened in 1995, the 42,000-square-foot, hands-on children's museum features exhibits about art, music, science, and invention. The facility encourages creative thinking as youngsters dig for dinosaur bones, paint, sculpt, draw, and make their own musical recordings.

GUARANTEED TO PUT A SMILE ON your face—and possibly elsewhere—Chattanooga's Riverbend Festival is a five-stage, nine-day celebration that includes live music, fancy dancing, and plenty of good eating. Each year, more than 500,000 people flock to the banks of the Tennessee River at Ross' Landing to hear stars such as B.B. King, James Brown, Tanya Tucker, and Willie Nelson perform on an elaborate floating stage.

ELVIS RARELY LEAVES THE BUILDING at this local bowling alley, where a glimpse of the King ranks right up there with a strike.

A T HISTORIC NIKKI'S, THE WAIT staff is always ready to serve up a sampling of the eatery's famous down-home fries, hamburgers, shrimp, and catfish.

F EEL LIKE STRUTTIN' YOUR STUFF? Then head to Chattanooga for the annual Bessie Smith Strut. The only part of the Riverbend Festival that takes place away from the water-front, the event is a lively mix of music and motion that turns M.L. King Boulevard into a massive dance floor. Featuring performances by such major blues artists as Albert King and Clarence "Gatemouth" Brown, the Bessie Smith Strut celebrates the life of the Chattanooga-born legend who, as a child, sang on the city's streets for coins before achieving international success as the Empress of the Blues.

WITH ALL THE TRAIN TALK IN Chattanooga, Robert Bernhardt may be the only conductor in town who doesn't shout "alllll aboard!" That's because, as leader of the Chat-tanooga Symphony, he's more concerned with tubas and trombones than wheels and whistles. Still, Bernhardt keeps the 80-member orchestra on track, steering them through a regular season of concerts at the Tivoli Theatre, along with special performances, such as the annual Fourth of July Pops in the Park concert at Chickamauga Battlefield.

WHETHER ASPIRING AMATEURS OR practiced professionals, local performers certainly have stage presence. The Chattanooga Ballet's annual production of the *Nutcracker* at the refurbished Tivoli Theatre is a holiday favorite (OPPOSITE TOP), as is the live nativity scene at the Collegedale Seventh-Day Adventist Church, where an assembly of angels take a much-deserved break (OPPOSITE BOTTOM). Back at the Tivoli, members of the Chattanooga Symphony prepare for another crowd-pleasing concert (ABOVE).

WHEN IT WAS COMPLETED IN 1909, the Grand Dome over the lobby of Terminal Station—now the Chattanooga Choo-Choo hotel—was the largest freestanding dome in the world (OPPOSITE). With a memorable dome of its own, the baroque Tivoli Theatre hosts performances by the city's symphony orchestra and ballet company, along with nationally known entertainers (LEFT). The elegantly refurbished theater, which was built in 1921, seats nearly 1,800.

FLIGHTS OF FANCY: A GROUP OF balloon enthusiasts prepare to rise to the occasion. With its beautiful landscape and breathtaking vistas, Chattanooga is a favorite among hot-air balloonists for much the same reason hang-gliders find the city a great place to hang out.

CHATTANOOGA

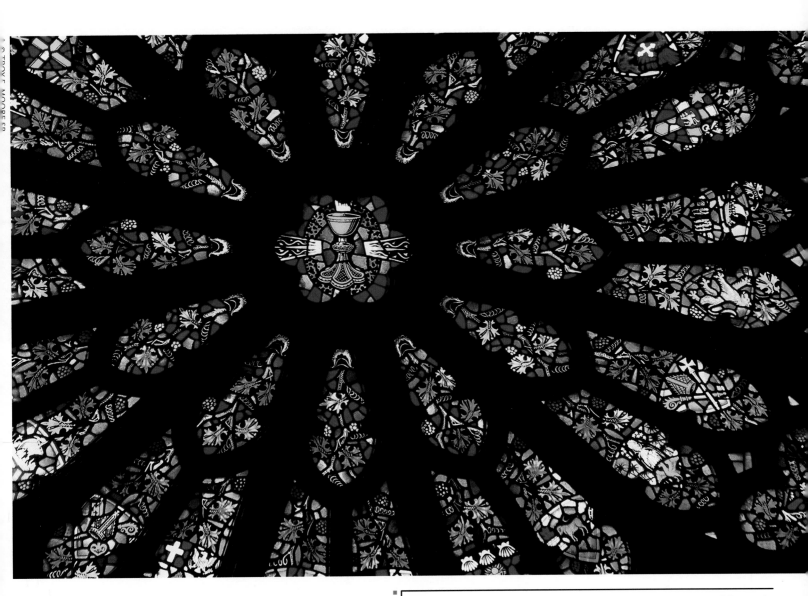

W ITH THE GLORIOUS MODEL NA-
ture provides, it's no wonder
local artisans create such beauty. Perhaps the maker of this stained-glass
window at the University of the South
in nearby Sewanee sought inspiration
from the priceless work of an anony-
mous spider.

RELIGION PLAYS AN IMPORTANT role in everyday life throughout the Chattanooga area. In Signal Mountain, a bough of golden leaves against a well-tended church evokes a feeling of quiet peace and amazing grace (PAGES 118 AND 119). And no matter where you are, donning your Sunday best is sure to elicit a smile (PAGES 120 AND 121).

W HETHER IT'S A COLLECTION OF hand-made votive candles covered in religious icons (PAGES 122 AND 123) or a series of metal sculptures in silhouette at a local craft show (PAGES 124 AND 125), Chattanoogans find creative ways to enliven ordinary spaces.

ITH ITS WIDE EXPANSES, THE Chattanooga-Hamilton County Bicentennial Library draws teenagers downtown to perfect their skateboarding technique. While one "sidewalk surfer" catches a concrete "wave" in front of the facility, another contemplates his next high-flying move.

CHATTANOOGA

TEAMWORK AND GOOD SPORTSMAN-
ship are part of the fabric of
Chattanooga life. Whether it's football
or softball, varsity or intramural, kids
and their families regularly pack the
city's many stadiums and ballparks.

AMERICA'S FAVORITE PASTIME has long been a Chattanooga mainstay. In fact, the city's Class AA team—the Lookouts—dates back to 1885, making it one of the oldest professional baseball clubs in the coun-try. Engel Stadium, the team's home, has its own claim to fame. Built in 1929, the facility is the oldest baseball park in the Southern League.

Fans who view the sport as an art form would certainly have appreci-ated a recent touring exhibit at the Hunter Museum, where *Present Echoes* by Washington, D.C., artist John Dreyfuss peppered the grounds with 19 bronze sculptures (PAGES 132 AND 133).

They say life imitates art, but the "stony" silence between two figures in the Hunter Museum's sculpture garden stands in stark contrast to this happy, real-life couple nestled in a willow love seat.

CHATTANOOGA

A POPULAR STOP FOR THOSE IN search of fresh rutabagas and radishes, the Chattanooga farmer's market features a bounteous selection of straight-from-the-field produce. Each Halloween, children from local day care centers are invited to pick out pumpkins and enjoy the "spooky" decorations (OPPOSITE). Elsewhere, autumn's colorful characters can be found hanging around in unexpected places, putting on a happy face or just standing watch over a garden of fall flowers.

CHATTANOOGA

THE RUSTIC BEAUTY OF EASTERN Tennessee surrounds the community of Dunlap, located about 30 mountainous miles north of Chattanooga in the Sequatchie Valley.

DEEP IN THE SEQUATCHIE VALLEY lie fertile fields, where dedicated farmers raise grapes and other crops. One of only two natural rift valleys in the world—the other being the Great Victoria in Africa—the Sequatchie extends some 125 miles in length, although it never exceeds five miles in width.

FOR DECADES, MIGRANT WORKERS from Guatamala, Mexico, and other points south have made their way to Dayton Mountain, just north of Chattanooga, where they help harvest the late-summer crop of tomatoes and other produce.

CREAM OF THE CROP: EACH YEAR,
Chattanooga-area farmers harvest a beautiful bounty. Luckily, the
fruits—and vegetables—of their labors
are readily available at area markets,
produce stands, and craft shows, where
vendors hawk everything from boiled
peanuts to homemade preserves
(PAGES 144-147).

LIKE STORYTELLING AND MOUNTAIN music, craft-making is an enduring part of southeast Tennessee culture. Each October, Chattanooga's Fall Color Cruise celebrates the vibrant foliage around the Grand Canyon of the Tennessee River with boat rides and a folk arts festival.

WHERE HAVE ALL THE COWBOYS gone? Well, you'll find some of them—along with their caricatures—in the Chattanooga area. Television and movie cowboy Walter Gilbreath, a native of a nearby northeast Alabama town, relishes his photo opportunity with James Arness of *Gunsmoke* fame (ABOVE). Gilbreath has also appeared with such screen legends as Roy Rogers, John Wayne, and Clayton "The Lone Ranger" Moore.

CHATTANOOGA

PICKIN' AND GRINNIN'? WELL, not in *this* case. But indigenous styles—from mountain music and country swing to bluegrass and gospel—have certainly put a smile on many a listener's face.

TWILIGHT'S LAST GLEAMING: From dusk to dawn, the light is always right in Chattanooga, and the fishing's not bad, either (PAGES 154-157).

Fireworks at a recent Riverbend Festival light up the evening sky over the Tennessee River (PAGES 158 AND 159). Along the historic water- front where Chattanooga was founded nearly two centuries ago, the city has begun to reinvent itself in a renaissance worth celebrating.

PROFILES IN EXCELLENCE

A LOOK AT THE CORPORATIONS, BUSINESSES, PROFESSIONAL GROUPS, AND COMMUNITY SERVICE ORGANIZATIONS THAT HAVE MADE THIS BOOK POSSIBLE. THEIR STORIES—OFFERING AN INFORMAL CHRONICLE OF THE LOCAL BUSINESS COMMUNITY—ARE ARRANGED ACCORDING TO THE DATE THEY WERE ESTABLISHED IN CHATTANOOGA.

AAA Courier Service ✳ ABB CE Power Products Manufacturing ✳ Adams Hilborne Mansion Inn & Restaurant ✳ Alexian Village of Tennessee ✳ Allied Arts of Greater Chattanooga ✳ American Manufacturing Company ✳ AmSouth Bancorporation ✳ Arthur Andersen ✳ Baker, Donelson, Bearman & Caldwell ✳ Ballet Tennessee/ Baker-Van Cura Ballet Centre ✳ BellSouth/BellSouth Mobility ✳ Bluff View Art District ✳ Brach & Brock Confections ✳ Cavalier Corporation ✳ The Center for Sports Medicine & Orthopaedics ✳ Chambliss, Bahner & Stophel, P.C. ✳ Chattanooga Area Chamber of Commerce ✳ Chattanooga Choo-Choo Holiday Inn ✳ Chattanooga Neighborhood Enterprise, Inc. ✳ Columbia/HCA Chattanooga Region ✳ Connecticut General Life Insurance Company, a CIGNA HealthCare Company ✳ Covenant College ✳ Daniel+Douglas+Norcross ✳ Docu-Shred ✳ DuPont Nylon-Chattanooga Plant ✳ Electric Power Board of Chattanooga ✳ Erlanger Health System ✳ Ernst & Young LLP ✳ e.spire ✳ First Tennessee Bank ✳ The Fletcher Bright Company ✳ Hunter Museum of American Art ✳ Insurance Planning & Service Company, Inc. ✳ Joseph Decosimo and Company, LLP ✳ The Krystal Company ✳ McKee Foods Corporation ✳ Memorial Hospital/Chattanooga Heart Institute ✳ Metropolitan Security, Inc. ✳ Miller & Martin ✳ Mountain City Realtors ✳ Petty & Landis, P.C. ✳ Provident Companies, Inc. ✳ Radisson Read House Hotel & Suites ✳ Rock-Tenn Company ✳ Southern Adventist University ✳ SunTrust Bank, Chattanooga, N.A. ✳ Tennessee Aquarium ✳ T.U. Parks Construction Company ✳ University of Tennessee at Chattanooga ✳ U.S. Xpress Enterprises, Inc. ✳ Volunteer Bank & Trust Company ✳ Wheland Foundry ✳ WUSY-FM/US-101 ✳

1847-1948

1847 Radisson Read House Hotel & Suites

1865 Cavalier Corporation

1867 Miller & Martin

1873 Wheland Foundry

1876 Chattanooga Area Chamber of Commerce

1880 BellSouth/BellSouth Mobility

1886 Chambliss, Bahner & Stophel, P.C.

1886 University of Tennessee at Chattanooga

1887 Connecticut General Life Insurance Company, a CIGNA HealthCare Company

1887 Provident Companies, Inc.

1888 ABB CE Power Products Manufacturing

1889 First Tennessee Bank

1891 Erlanger Health System

1892 Southern Adventist University

1898 American Manufacturing Company

1906 Brach & Brock Confections

1912 SunTrust Bank, Chattanooga, N.A.

1917 Rock-Tenn Company

1927 The Fletcher Bright Company

1928 Baker, Donelson, Bearman & Caldwell

1932 The Krystal Company

1934 McKee Foods Corporation

1935 Electric Power Board of Chattanooga

1936 Alexian Village of Tennessee

1944 T.U. Parks Construction Company

1947 The Center for Sports Medicine & Orthopaedics

1948 DuPont Nylon-Chattanooga Plant

Radisson Read House Hotel & Suites

WHAT DO WINSTON CHURCHILL, DIZZY DEAN, ANDREW JOHNSON, Ronald Reagan, Gloria Swanson, Bob Hope, William McKinley, Gary Cooper, Benny Goodman, Gene Autry, Rutherford B. Hayes, Richard Nixon, Al Capone, and General Tom Thumb all have in common? They've all been guests at the Radisson Read House, the venerable Chattanooga institution whose

history dates to 1847. Those notables understood what discerning guests today have learned: A stay at the Radisson Read House is a visit with history.

More than simply a beautiful place to spend a comfortable night or two, Radisson Read House invites its guests to walk hallways once strolled by presidents, world leaders, and the rich and famous. To dine in the style of those elegant, bygone days, or hold gatherings in unique settings that recall the history-changing meetings that have been held there. To sip a scotch in the Green Room, enjoy a cool drink on the open-air veranda, or taste a fresh-brewed coffee while admiring one of the hotel's many murals—all while soaking in the unique sense of place that only a stay in the Radisson Read House can deliver to the Chattanooga visitor.

The Radisson Read House is a masterpiece of antebellum architecture that has been renovated to reflect its original grandeur. Steeped in the past, no discussion of the Radisson Read House would be complete without a brief look at the people and times the stately manse has witnessed.

REMEMBERING THE PAST

The hotel opened as the Crutchfield House in 1847. The Thomas Crutchfield family entered the inn keeping business just as the Western & Atlantic rail lines prepared to link Chattanooga with Atlanta and other commercial centers in the Deep South. The Crutchfields built their inn directly across from the rail terminal, establishing a lively business from the start. The trains arrived in 1850 and brought an economic boom to Chattanooga.

By January 1861, the times were taking an ominous tone. On his way home to Mississippi after resigning from the U.S. Senate, Jefferson Davis stopped in Chattanooga and spoke to the crowd gathered in the hotel lobby. When Davis finished, William Crutchfield, brother of the owner, jumped up on the counter. From his podium, Crutchfield reviled

Davis as a traitor and military despot. Audience loyalties were divided and passions flared. Bloodshed was narrowly averted when Thomas Crutchfield Jr., a Southern sympathizer, hustled his brother away.

Not long after that incident, Thomas Crutchfield sold the hotel. The new owners soon had great cause to regret their purchase. By 1863, the Civil War had engulfed Chattanooga, snuffing out civilian commerce. The hotel was the first building in Chattanooga to be occupied by the Union forces and was converted into a Union hospital in 1863. The hotel withstood the ravages of the entire war, only to face a calamitous fire in 1867.

With virtually nothing left of the previous structure, Dr. John T. Read and his son, Samuel, rebuilt

THE RADISSON READ HOUSE IS A MASTERPIECE OF CIVIL WAR-ERA ARCHITECTURE, AND IS LISTED IN THE NATIONAL REGISTER OF HISTORIC PLACES (LEFT).

THE LOBBY IS BEAUTIFULLY DEFINED BY ITS SOARING COLUMNS OF QUARTER-SAWED WALNUT (RIGHT).

▲ QUALITY PHOTO

CLOCKWISE FROM TOP:
A WEALTH OF COMFORTS INCLUDING
A WET BAR, CABLE TV, AND COMPLIMEN-
TARY COFFEE MAKERS ARE PROVIDED IN
STATELY TWO ROOM SUITES.

FOR THE ULTIMATE IN GOURMET DIN-
ING, STEAKS AT THE GREEN ROOM IS
A LANDMARK IN CHATTANOOGA.

THE SILVER BALLROOM IS UNMATCHED
WITH ITS HAND CARVED AND GILDED
MOLDING AND STERLING SILVER
WATERFORD CRYSTAL CHANDELIERS.

the hotel in 1871 and gave the establishment the name it bears to this day. The Reads persevered through Reconstruction, and, with Samuel at the helm, the hotel gradually earned a prestigious reputation. The Read House became the address of distinction for out-of-town visitors.

In 1926, the Read family replaced the original structure with the present 10-story brick and terra-cotta building. Designed in the Georgian style by Holabird and Roche, it was constructed with lavish appointments now too costly to duplicate: terrazzo floors inlaid with marble, paneling of quarter-sawed walnut, carved and gilded woodwork, mirrors recessed in massive arches, a ballroom with a 25-foot ceiling, and a lobby beautifully defined by its soaring columns. In 1977, the hotel was included in the National Register of Historic Places as a prime example of period architecture and decorative art.

A MEMORABLE PLACE TO MEET

Today, the Radisson Read House features 137 two-room suites and 100 finely appointed standard rooms. The historic quality is complemented with modern amenities, including specialty shops, an outdoor pool, and in-room conveniences such as coffeemakers, wet bars, cable television, and free HBO.

The elegant Silver Ballroom offers more than 3,700 square feet of meeting space. With its hand-carved molding and sterling silver chandeliers, adorned with sparkling Waterford crystal, the Silver Ballroom provides a truly unique setting for any size party. With more than 16,000 total square feet of meeting space, the Read House is versatile in its function space, and its staff is highly experienced in catering meetings, from an intimate gathering of five to a formal reception for 500.

For the ultimate in gourmet dining, Steaks at the Green Room— which serves the finest USDA prime beef—is a Chattanooga landmark. The gourmet meals are as spectacular as the luxurious Victorian surround-

ings in which they are served. A slightly less formal meal can be had at Madelyne's Tavern, a warm and friendly room where a delicious breakfast, lunch, or dinner can be enjoyed.

Located in the center of downtown Chattanooga, the Radisson Read House is minutes away from restaurants, shopping, attractions, and the Convention and Trade Center. The electric trolley shuttle service stops at the Radisson Read House, offering guests a relaxing ride to their downtown Chattanooga destinations.

A brilliant blending of the past and the present, the Radisson Read House affords the discerning traveler a chance to relive history while enjoying all the modern amenities of a world-class hotel.

BILL GARRY'S BUSINESS CARD SAYS IT ALL: THE NEW CAVALIER. BROUGHT back from the brink of dissolution, Chattanooga's longest-operating manufacturer stands today on solid ground, armed with capital, an enthusiastic workforce, and a committed management team that has already produced exciting results. Cavalier Corporation, which makes cold-drink vending machines and glass-door coolers, can point with pride to a number of recent accomplishments: an entirely new and much more efficient manufacturing facility, continued technological advances in products, and increased sales, including some in such unexpected places as Russia and Argentina.

The rebirth of Cavalier mirrors the renaissance that has taken place in Chattanooga. The basic ingredients of both revitalizations are, in fact, the same: public/private partnerships that have coalesced to form sound business plans that generate growth.

In Cavalier's case, the road back began in 1995. That year, Norman Sarkisian, Cavalier's owner, joined forces with city, state, and federal officials to see how the company could be reenergized to boost stagnant sales and lagging profitability. The revitalization team included the not-for-profit Southeast Local Development Corporation, the U.S. government's Economic Development Agency, Tennessee Valley Authority (TVA), SunTrust Bank, the engineering firm of Campbell and Associates, and city and state leaders. Their efforts resulted in a plan to completely renovate Cavalier's manufacturing capabilities and to provide favorable loans from TVA and SunTrust to finance the project. Today, those plans have been realized.

Garry, president of Cavalier, says, "The transformation is nothing short of total. We have rebuilt our manufacturing base, instilled renewed confidence in our employees and our customers, and positioned ourselves to take part in the growing global marketplace for cold soft drinks. We are a new Cavalier."

A CHATTANOOGA LANDMARK

A look at Cavalier Corporation's long history reveals a company determined to survive, despite the changes of the region's economy. The firm began in 1865 as Loomis and Hart, a sawmill on the banks of the Tennessee River founded by Union army veteran J.F. Loomis. After some years in business, Loomis and his partner, J.A. Hart, came up with the idea of using the scrap wood their mill produced to make furniture. Production began in 1875, and soon, furniture output overtook the milling operation and the sawmill was shut down.

In 1905, the company was purchased by Gaston Raoul, who had also acquired the rather pointedly named Odorless Refrigerator Company, a manufacturer of small wooden refrigerators. The combined firm—called the Tennessee Furniture Company— soon became the second-largest manufacturer of wooden refrigerators in the nation. In 1923, the company introduced a memorable name for its best-selling product: the Cavalier. The name caught on so well that the firm became better known as the maker of the Cavalier than as the

CAVALIER CORPORATION'S CURRENT OFFICE RENOVATIONS REPRESENT THE COMPANY'S COMMITMENT TO THE CHATTANOOGA AREA.

THE VIPROS 357, CAVALIER'S NEWEST TURRET PUNCH, IS A STATE-OF-THE-ART SHEET METAL MACHINE.

Tennessee Furniture Company. In 1938, the firm made it official, changing its name to Cavalier Corporation.

The arrival of electric refrigeration, however, changed the company's fortunes. Though the firm still manufactured and sold furniture, Cavalier saw its ice refrigerator sales dwindle to literally nothing by 1938. Raoul foresaw the change and set out to put the company's future on more solid ground. A major turning point came in 1934, when he secured a contract with the Coca-Cola Company to produce open-type ice coolers and electric well coolers. Cavalier's products were a big hit with Coca-Cola bottlers, and the company did very well—even with an interruption to convert to defense production during World War II.

Several years after the war, in 1949, Cavalier teamed with Coke to change the way consumers purchased soft drinks. Cavalier developed a coin-operated cold-drink vending machine. Coke and Cavalier turned this invention into a huge business—by the late 1950s, the cold bottle sold in Cavalier's machines represented 50 percent of the volume of Coke bottlers.

During the next three decades, company ownership changed hands many times. Some of these sales did not turn out well for Cavalier, and the company was eventually forced to file for reorganization under Chapter 11. In August 1987, the assets of the Cavalier Company were sold to the Beacon Group of Bloomfield, headed by Sarkisian.

QUALITY REMAINS THE WATCHWORD

Despite the company's many adversities, Cavalier's employees never flinched in their commitment to produce quality equipment. To this day, the company enjoys a reputation for manufacturing quality products—a reputation it backs in writing with a seven-year warranty on its refrigeration systems, the industry's longest.

Garry, who joined the company in 1996, attributes the firm's long life and reputation for quality to the resiliency and determination of its workforce. "In all my years in manufacturing, I've never seen such a remarkable group of people. They have withstood some pretty tough times and, through it all, never gave up, always worked hard to put out top-notch products. I can't tell you how gratifying it is for me now to see that their fortitude has paid off. That they, like Cavalier itself, stand today on the brink of a new era, an era marked by growth and opportunity for everyone involved."

WITH MORE THAN 20 MACHINES IN THE MANUFACTURING AREA, CAVALIER IS CAPABLE OF PRODUCING 115 VENDERS PER DAY (LEFT).

CAVALIER ASSEMBLES ALL OF ITS PRODUCTS ON SITE IN ITS NEWLY RENOVATED BUILIDNG, ASSURING THE HIGHEST POSSIBLE QUALITY (RIGHT).

HAVING CONVERTED FROM LIQUID PAINT TO THIS AUTOMATED POWDER COATING OPERATION, CAVALIER IS AT THE FOREFRONT IN FINISHING TECHNOLOGY (LEFT).

THE "RETRO-50S" COOLER IS A NICHE IN CAVALIER'S VENDING MACHINE LINE (RIGHT).

Back in 1867, when T.M. Burkett founded what is now Miller & Martin, he undoubtedly had little idea that his tiny local law firm would one day be recognized for representing multinational clients competing in the global marketplace. How Miller & Martin made that transformation is a testament to the ongoing adaptability and progressive thinking that have always been the hallmarks of the

firm. Still strongly rooted in its Chattanooga heritage, Miller & Martin has grown as its clients have grown, taking the firm into virtually every corner of the world and many of the most challenging areas of contemporary law.

Today, Miller & Martin is a full-service law firm with more than 100 attorneys in 20 areas of practice operating out of offices in Chattanooga, Atlanta, and Nashville. Among the firm's many legal services are corporate securities, mergers and acquisitions, labor and employment, antitrust, litigation, real estate, finance, health care, environmental, tax, ERISA and employee benefits, estate planning, intellectual property, bankruptcy, international law, financial institutions, and immigration.

A Progressive Firm

Miller & Martin has long been recognized as a firm with visionary thinkers and insightful

ideas—corporatewide traits that have benefited both the Chattanooga community and the firm's clients.

In the community, the firm's forward thinking has helped energize and shape the rebirth of downtown Chattanooga. Examples of Miller & Martin's efforts in that regard abound. Miller Plaza and

Miller Park—a project that helped launch Chattanooga's downtown revitalization—are named after the late Burkett Miller, to memorialize his visionary and generous spirit. Similarly, the Hitching Visitors Center at the Tennessee Aquarium and the Waterhouse Pavilion in Miller Plaza both honor Miller &

MILLER & MARTIN WAS FOUNDED IN 1867 AND TODAY IS RECOGNIZED FOR ITS REPRESENTATION OF CLIENTS COMPETING IN THE GLOBAL MARKETPLACE.

NAMED AFTER MILLER & MARTIN PARTNER H. JAMES HITCHING, THE HITCHING VISITORS CENTER SERVES AS A WELCOME STATION TO THOSE VISITING THE CHATTANOOGA AREA AND RECOGNIZES HITCHING'S INVOLVEMENT IN COMMUNITY EFFORTS TO REVITALIZE CHATTANOOGA'S DOWNTOWN ALONG THE RIVERFRONT.

ROBERT C. BOYER

Martin namesakes: H. James Hitching and the late James F. Waterhouse, in recognition of their civic leadership and contributions to the community.

The firm's tradition of public service remains strong today, with many Miller & Martin lawyers involved in civic and charitable activities, including the Lyndhurst Foundation, Tonya Memorial Foundation, United Way of Greater Chattanooga, Allied Arts, and Tennessee Aquarium. These foundations and organizations are playing a major role in revitalizing downtown Chattanooga, and Miller & Martin continues to contribute vital support through its distinguished roster of leaders in civic affairs and public service.

Growing with Its Clients

Not surprisingly, those very same leaders are often key advisers to some of the Chattanooga area's most prominent companies, including soft drink bottling, manufacturing, textile, food service, and health care businesses. Valued for their seasoned advice, experience, and proactive thinking, Miller & Martin attorneys are helping these and other large firms located in the Southeast and elsewhere capitalize on the emerging global economy, weather the ebb and flow of regulation and deregulation, and harness the synergies of corporate acquisitions.

Such complex challenges have been the catalyst for Miller & Martin's strong growth. A look at some of the firm's recent work underscores Miller & Martin's vast and growing breadth of experience, increasingly global practice, and commitment to expanding its capabilities and services to meet the needs of its clients.

In the recent past, for example, Miller & Martin has helped a large number of foreign companies set up operations in the Southeast; handled the acquisition of a French manufacturing company with revenues in excess of $200 million; served as lead counsel for a Big Five accounting firm in litigation resulting in the successful defense of a nationwide class action discrimination lawsuit; completed domestic and international acquisitions on behalf of a client that were valued in excess of $3.1 billion; prepared and implemented a leave

policy under the Family and Medical Leave Act (FMLA) for a national corporation involving a corporatewide policy and several separate policies for facilities located in states having state laws granting more extensive leave rights than FMLA; and handled the international intellectual property work for several companies with famous brand names.

A World View

The firm has also moved in other ways to dramatically expand its capabilities. Miller & Martin has become a member of the World Law Group, an international network of more than 40 law firms from approximately 30 countries. The primary purpose of the World Law Group is to develop, maintain, and coordinate the capabilities and resources required to provide quality legal services efficiently to international clients no matter where they are headquartered.

Additionally, Miller & Martin has built a technological infrastructure that enables the firm to respond rapidly and efficiently to client needs. With all offices electronically interconnected, the firm's lawyers can work on the same document with-

out having to be in the same office. This seamless operation allows Miller & Martin to instantly tap the firm's deep levels of experience, offering clients fast, comprehensive responses.

Service Oriented

Miller & Martin continues to distinguish itself through service. The firm is dedicated to providing quality legal services that are cost effective and offer real value to the client. Furthermore, Miller & Martin encourages its attorneys to provide personal service, respond quickly, and offer the open access clients need to stay abreast of an ever changing marketplace. Teamwork and cooperation are the operative words when describing Miller & Martin's approach to project management.

Moreover, Miller & Martin facilitates the development of its legal staff, offers incentives that contribute to the staff's stability, and recruits and trains quality law school graduates.

With its blend of well-rounded experience, long-standing community preeminence, emphasis on service, and world view, Miller & Martin is uniquely positioned to help its clients have a lasting global impact in the 21st century.

MILLER & MARTIN PARTNER BURKETT MILLER'S VISION FOR AN IMPROVED DOWNTOWN CHATTANOOGA LED TO THE DEVELOPMENT OF MILLER PLAZA AND MILLER PARK. THE WATERHOUSE PAVILION IN MILLER PLAZA IS NAMED FOR PARTNER JAMES F. WATERHOUSE, WHO FURTHERED MILLER'S EFFORTS BY TAKING AN ACTIVE ROLE IN THE DEVELOPMENT OF THE PLAZA AND PARK COMPLEX.

ROBERT C. BOYER

AFTER THE CIVIL WAR, NUMEROUS IRONWORKS SPRANG UP IN THE Chattanooga area. Railroads, water transportation, and access to raw materials made the city a likely choice for the manufacturing of iron. ✳ Among the soldiers who returned to the area after the war was George W. Wheland, who in 1866 built a foundry and machinery repair shop (then called the Wheland Company) in Athens, Tennessee. After moving to Chattanooga in 1873, Wheland's business expanded to include the production of sawmills, gristmills, and waterwheels, and it eventually grew into the South's first large-scale production foundry.

Today, Wheland Foundry, a subsidiary of North American Royalties, Inc. (NAR), is the largest independent producer of gray iron automotive brake castings in the United States, with more than half of all cars and light trucks built domestically containing one or more Wheland-made castings.

Wheland employs 2,000 people at its five foundries and produces up to 200,000 castings in a single day. On an average day, almost 5 million pounds of material are molded into 200 types of castings, including brake drums, rotors, hubs, clutch plates, calipers, anchors, support brackets, and flywheels.

COMMITTED TO RECYCLING

Because it uses scrap iron, the foundry industry was a pioneer in the recycling movement. Wheland continues this tradition by recycling an average of 2,000 tons of scrap metal each day. Wheland's commitment to the environment was recognized recently by the Tennessee Association of Business, which presented Wheland with its Excellence in Solid Waste Management Award in 1997.

The continual development of new products and better production techniques has enabled Wheland to maintain its long history of promoting the economic progress of Chattanooga. Through the involvement of Wheland management in a leadership role in the Chattanooga Manufacturers Association, and through the establishment of a local industrial park, called NARPARK, the company is working with the city to attract business development.

NARPARK is a prime example of the revitalization of a brownfield site—an old, abandoned industrial site located in an urban area. NAR saw this site as an opportunity for Wheland Foundry, and thus decided to buy the property because of its potential to bring jobs and economic growth to the area. Today, NARPARK is fully developed and provides more than 200 jobs. Wheland Foundry also uses a portion of NARPARK as a weighing station for trucks delivering supplies and raw materials to the company's plant.

Wheland's involvement in civic, educational, and philanthropic activities continues to have a positive impact on the city and region. In 1996, Wheland donated the Harris-Johnson Community Park to the City of Chattanooga for the company's neighbors' recreational use. Other specific involvement includes leadership in the United Way, Hamilton County Partners in Education Program, Tennessee Aquarium, Alton Park Health Center, and Creative Discovery Museum. In addition, Wheland has been a leader in the local historic preservation movement, with its restoration of the former Chattanooga Carnegie Library (now the company's headquarters), as well as the Dome Building, a Chattanooga landmark and original site of *The Chattanooga Times* newspaper.

"For more than 130 years, Wheland Foundry has been a key player in making Chattanooga a good place to live and conduct business," says Gordon P. Street Jr., chief executive officer of NAR. "Our continued mission is to maintain this leadership role."

TODAY, WHELAND FOUNDRY, A SUBSIDIARY OF NORTH AMERICAN ROYALTIES, INC. (NAR), IS THE LARGEST INDEPENDENT PRODUCER OF GRAY IRON AUTOMOTIVE BRAKE CASTINGS IN THE UNITED STATES, WITH MORE THAN HALF OF ALL CARS AND LIGHT TRUCKS BUILT DOMESTICALLY CONTAINING ONE OR MORE WHELAND-MADE CASTINGS (LEFT).

WHELAND HAS BEEN A LEADER IN THE LOCAL HISTORIC PRESERVATION MOVEMENT, WITH ITS RESTORATION OF THE FORMER CHATTANOOGA CARNEGIE LIBRARY (NOW THE COMPANY'S HEADQUARTERS) AS WELL AS THE DOME BUILDING, A CHATTANOOGA LANDMARK AND ORIGINAL SITE OF *The Chattanooga Times* NEWSPAPER (RIGHT).

SINCE ITS FOUNDING AS CHATTANOOGA UNIVERSITY IN 1886, THE University of Tennessee at Chattanooga (UTC) has borne the name of the city it serves. UTC meets the educational, intellectual, and cultural needs of the community, as well as being an integral partner in the future achievements of the region. ✳ "I believe that the people of this community want UTC to lead, to do even more," says Bill Stacy, UTC

chancellor since August 1997. "They want our brain power to help solve community issues. That's a wonderful demand. And it comes back to the partnership that the community has with this campus." UTC has always enjoyed a close relationship with the city. Private funds from the community enabled the institution to open its doors to the first 1,500 college students in Chattanooga in 1886. For 83 years, the school operated as a private university that nurtured a strong liberal arts tradition while at the same time working with the local business community.

In 1969, the University of Chattanooga and Chattanooga City College, a historically African-American institution, combined and joined the University of Tennessee system as one of its four primary, multidisciplinary campuses. UTC's enrollment has grown to more than 8,600 students representing not only Chattanooga, but every Tennessee county, most states, and numerous foreign countries. With a student/faculty ratio of 18-to-1, students receive individual attention that is instructive while allowing them to experience a great level of independence.

EDUCATING
CHATTANOOGA'S LEADERS

UTC offers a broad curriculum of majors and concentrations with more than 100 bachelor's and 46 master's degree programs offered by the Colleges of Arts and Science, Education and Applied Professional Studies, Engineering and Computer Science, and Health and Human Services, as well as the School of Business Administration. New academic programs have been developed in response to community needs and goals, including a master's degree in environmental science and a forthcoming doctorate in environmental engineering. Stretching beyond the traditional classroom, UTC encompasses the entire community. Evening classes and noncredit courses are

popular, and the university's art, music, and theater programs are important to the city's cultural offerings.

UTC is home to the Center of Excellence for Computer Applications and nine chairs of excellence supporting innovation in teaching and research. The Southeast Center for Education in the Arts helps regional schools implement discipline-based arts education programs in music, theater, and the visual arts. The UTC Challenger Center offers students the opportunity to explore the wonders of math and science through team-building space mission simulations.

The campus is assisted in its academic mission by the University of Chattanooga Foundation Inc., whose trustees include the civic, business, government, and cultural leaders of the Chattanooga community. With an endowment exceeding $77 million, the foundation supports scholarships, professorships, and academic enhancement programs that otherwise might not be possible.

"As our business climate changed, so did Chattanooga. And always, there was Chattanooga's university, growing with the city, changing as it changed," says Ruth Holmberg, chairman of the *Chattanooga Times* and a trustee of the University of Chattanooga Foundation. "Our city and our university are inseparable."

CLOCKWISE FROM TOP:
THE UNIVERSITY OF TENNESSEE AT CHATTANOOGA (UTC) OFFERS A BROAD CURRICULUM OF MAJORS AND CONCENTRATIONS WITH MORE THAN 100 BACHELOR'S AND 46 MASTER'S DEGREE PROGRAMS.

PRIVATE FUNDS FROM THE COMMUNITY ENABLED THE INSTITUTION TO OPEN ITS DOORS TO THE FIRST 1,500 COLLEGE STUDENTS IN CHATTANOOGA IN 1886.

STRETCHING BEYOND THE TRADITIONAL CLASSROOM, UTC ENCOMPASSES THE ENTIRE COMMUNITY.

JOE BENTON

ROBIN HOOD

I T SEEMS AS IF EVERYONE AGREES: THE RIVER CITY RENAISSANCE HAS BEEN nothing short of miraculous. In fewer than three decades, Chattanooga—once called "the dirtiest city in America," mired in a stagnant economy and weighted with a crumbling infrastructure and dilapidated downtown—has transformed itself into a fresh-faced, growing, and vibrant community pointed in a new direction. In doing so, this medium-sized

city on the banks of the Tennessee River has drawn the attention and praise of leaders from all corners of the world.

In fact, many of those leaders have come to Chattanooga to study firsthand the processes and partnerships that have helped make this remarkable transformation happen. They've been joined by an army of reporters and news organizations chronicling the progress that's been made in the city. As a result, Chattanooga has received an impressive number of accolades from a variety of publications. Among the many tributes: *U.S. News & World Report* picked Chattanooga from all the other cities in the world as one of the Six Cities That Work; *Family Fun* magazine named Chattanooga one of its Top 10 Family Vacation Cities alongside cities like San Antonio, Washington, Chicago, and Seattle; and *Utne Reader* labeled the River City one of America's Ten Most

Enlightened Towns, a designation earned by cities "making a special effort to foster connectedness and contentment among all the people who live in them."

A NEW CHALLENGE

And yet, despite all the accomplishments and widely diverse accolades (or, perhaps, because of

them), the River City Renaissance is about to take up a new challenge.

Jim Kennedy, chief executive officer of the Chattanooga Area Chamber of Commerce, put it this way: "All the fantastic work that's been done by RiverValley Partners, the Chamber of Commerce, and countless public/private partnerships has turned Chattanooga around and made us a shining example of how to successfully begin and foster the revitalization of a midsize city. Now we're ready to take those efforts to a new level."

During the next several years, the Chamber will squarely address the issue of economic development in two ways: by encouraging companies to locate their operations here and by nurturing the growth of the businesses already in Chattanooga. Both of these initiatives will hinge on the community's strongest attribute: the truly unique sense of cooperation and partnership that exists here between the business community, local government officials, civic leaders, and the public. It's a relationship that aims to enhance every aspect of this community's quality of life for all its residents.

"No other city in America," Kennedy asserts, "has come as far as we have to bring its diverse constituencies together to reach consensus, form public policy, and implement plans."

STARTING WITH THE TENNESSEE AQUARIUM, WHICH HAS BEEN A CATALYST FOR THE ENTIRE DOWNTOWN REVITALIZATION, CHATTANOOGA HAS INVESTED HEAVILY IN ITS CENTRAL CITY (TOP).

CHATTANOOGA IS A FRESH-FACED, GROWING, AND VIBRANT COMMUNITY POINTED IN A NEW DIRECTION (BOTTOM).

A Time of Great Opportunity

Chattanoogans see the end of this century and the beginning of the next as a time of tremendous opportunity for the area. Because of the unique cooperation between the various interests within this community, Chattanooga is poised to make even bigger strides in the next three decades. The area's charge is to use those cooperative forces to further build the economy, foster equity among its citizens, and develop the symbiotic relationship between commerce, industry, urban design, housing, education, transportation, and public spaces—all the societal linchpins that join and hold together the framework of this or any other community.

The revitalization of Chattanooga's downtown is an example of how this holistic approach can work. Starting with the Tennessee Aquarium, which has been a catalyst for the entire downtown revitalization, the community has invested heavily in its central city. This effort was accomplished through community visioning, public/private partner-ships, and the cooperation of many interests—business, transportation, development, and public housing—all of whom have benefited from the rewards of downtown's rebirth. Now the community is in the process of applying what it has already learned about revitalization to new projects in other areas of the city.

New Projects Moving Forward

Two of those projects are well under way. The first is an ambitious renaissance beginning to take place within the city's Southside, 640 acres of blighted land on the southern end of Chattanooga's downtown. The second focuses on revitalizing four square miles in the city's inner suburban ring anchored by Eastgate Mall—the area's oldest mall, long in decline. Both projects have incorporated community-based visioning efforts that have helped define their content and scope. Already, public/private partnerships have formed and the revitalization process has begun, taking infrastructure that had been all but abandoned and making it productive and vital once again.

A Standard of Quality

The success of these new projects—as well as those completed and proposed for the future—rests in part on the Chattanooga area's high standards for quality development. "We have been true to a high standard of quality in our development," Kennedy says. "We have to continue to set the bar high and apply those standards to all facets of our economic development activities.

"We also have to be careful to avoid becoming myopically focused on Chattanooga and neglecting to see the bigger regional picture. Chattanooga is no longer an isolated city in the Mid-South. We're strategically located in one of the fastest-growing regions in this nation. Opportunities abound. We need to make sure that we take part in those opportunities in ways that benefit Chattanooga and strengthen our relationship with the entire region."

Based on the area's past successes and willingness to look boldly to the future, the River City Renaissance may, indeed, have only just begun.

As a medium-sized city on the banks of the Tennessee River, Chattanooga has drawn the attention and praise of leaders from all corners of the world.

NEW TECHNOLOGY HAS ALWAYS BEEN A LITTLE DAUNTING, AS THE VERY first subscribers to the East Tennessee Telephone Company—one of the forerunners of today's BellSouth—found on July 9, 1880, the first day of telephone service for Chattanooga residents. One can only imagine how those people would react to today's technological wonders—many of which have been pioneered by BellSouth and its

affiliates. Headquartered in Atlanta, BellSouth provides an array of telecommunications services in nine southeastern states. The company serves more than 21 million local telephone lines, including more than 2.6 million in Tennessee.

INVESTING IN A RELIABLE INFRASTRUCTURE

To ensure the reliability and integrity of its services, BellSouth invests approximately $350 million annually to grow and modernize its Tennessee infrastructure, and to maintain and add backup capabilities. The company has built-in redundancies (such as its own back-up power supply), self-diagnostic equipment, and around-the-clock system monitoring, all helping to ensure uninterrupted service to customers. Additionally, BellSouth's network infrastructure features leading-edge technology, such as widespread deployment of fiber-optic facilities and digital switching in every exchange. In Chattanooga, for example, where millions of calls are made daily, BellSouth has installed some 50,000 miles of fiber-optic lines.

In addition to its state-of-the-art telephony capabilities, BellSouth is poised to be a major player in other emerging technologies. Changes in state and federal law are opening the

way for BellSouth to provide worldwide long-distance services from both standard and cellular phones, offer home entertainment services, and participate in the research and development of the next generation of telecommunications equipment.

"Our aim is to be world class across the board—not just in voice technology, but in video and data, as well," explains Patsy Hazlewood, regional director in Chattanooga.

CONNECTING WITH THE COMMUNITY

BellSouth is also using its telecommunications know-how to provide special services to the community. A prime example is BellSouth's

partnership with the Tennessee Department of Education, connecting the state's elementary, middle, and high schools to the Internet. As part of the program—called ConnecTEN—the schools are using BellSouth's Integrated Services Digital Network (ISDN) for fast and easy connection to the Internet, and are receiving the benefit of $1.7 million in annual discounts. One result: inner-city schools in Chattanooga, which can run short of educational resources, offer their students complete access to the World Wide Web. This Internet access is transforming the way teachers teach and children learn, and is yet another example of how BellSouth is helping the community grow.

S INCE 1985, BELLSOUTH MOBILITY HAS BEEN HELPING PEOPLE STAY IN touch throughout the Chattanooga area by providing the latest in wireless communication services, including advanced digital technology. Just as important, BellSouth Mobility is also committed to staying in touch with the community it serves by sponsoring projects and initiatives that strengthen the social fabric that binds people together.

"Futurists and trend spotters have long said that high tech should translate into 'high touch.' That is, advanced technology should allow individuals to more easily reach out to one another and form the bonds that create community," says Darda Williams, general manager of BellSouth Mobility of Chattanooga. "At BellSouth Mobility, we take this premise seriously, and believe it is our responsibility to reach out to the community–not just by providing superior wireless communication service, but also helping to ensure that key human services are available to sustain a strong community."

HIGH-TECH COMMITMENT

The first wireless communication company in Chattanooga to offer digital technology, BellSouth Mobility has taken mobile communications to a whole new level by offering advanced services like Caller ID, Numeric Paging, Digital Voice Mail, and Single Nationwide Roaming Rate, in addition to standard voice communication service.

"Thanks to the timesaving features made possible by digital technology, a small handset now provides virtually the same services as an entire room of office equipment. We call it Digital Freedom, because this technology provides our customers with the freedom to be extremely productive, no matter where they are," Williams says. "And, thanks to dual-mode technology—whereby a user's handset automatically switches from digital to analog mode, depending on the environment in which it is operating—BellSouth Mobility offers its customers the largest coverage area in the Southeast."

HIGH-TOUCH RESULTS

In the community, BellSouth Mobility is a strong advocate for education and programs benefiting young people because, Williams says, this is where the future lies.

"We want children who grow up in Chattanooga to stay here and contribute their talents to the whole community. The best way to make this happen is to ensure that the community has something to offer them in return," she says.

Combining its interest in the arts and education, BellSouth Mobility sponsors an art class at White Oak Elementary School. The company pays the salary of the art teacher who runs the class, and provides art supplies as a Christmas present each year. BellSouth Mobility employees are also encouraged to volunteer at the school throughout the year.

BellSouth Mobility is also one of the original sponsors of the Tennessee Aquarium, a key educational resource for area children. The company's focus on providing educational opportunities for the entire community has also included involvement with Allied Arts, a local program promoting the arts, including music, dance, painting, and sculpture. BellSouth Mobility is a key supporter of Chattanooga's Little Theater, which produces live dramatic performances for the entire family, and its work with Chattanooga's Urban League is designed to ensure that all segments of the population have an equal opportunity to share in what the community has to offer. In these and many other ways, BellSouth Mobility helps to bring the community together.

THE FIRST TO OFFER DIGITAL WIRELESS COMMUNICATIONS SERVICES IN THE CHATTANOOGA AREA, BELLSOUTH MOBILITY IS COMMITTED TO PROVIDING THE LATEST TECHNOLOGY ENABLING ITS CUSTOMERS TO STAY ON THE CUTTING EDGE OF TELECOMMUNICATIONS.

Chambliss, Bahner & Stophel, P.C.

FORMED WHEN TWO OF CHATTANOOGA'S LEADING AND OLDEST LAW FIRMS combined their practices, Chambliss, Bahner & Stophel, P.C. is committed to providing high-quality, timely services in meeting the diverse and broad-based legal needs of its individual and corporate clients. In 1886, Alexander W. Chambliss, who later served on the Tennessee Supreme Court as chief justice, began the firm's continu-

ing tradition of assisting its clients to achieve their objectives—no matter where the clients are located or how wide ranging their interests may be.

CLIENT COMMITMENT

Chambliss, Bahner & Stophel has changed considerably over the years, adapting and growing to meet ever changing client needs. The firm takes great pride in its ability to represent the interests of businesses as they enter and compete in new and larger markets, whether regional, national, or international. The firm's commitment to its clients is evidenced in its representation of a family that began making Little Debbie snack cakes in the 1960s and guided McKee Foods Corporation to its position as the leading

producer of snack cake products in the United States; and by the firm's representation of a group of high school classmates who started Astec Industries in 1972 and transformed it into a publicly held company that is one of the world's leading manufacturers of aggregate-processing and road-paving equipment.

Today, the firm practices in areas of modern-day importance, including patents and other intellectual property, health care, labor and employment, business planning, acquisitions, and all aspects of litigation. Additionally, the firm stays abreast of the latest regulations, issues, and trends related to a wide array of legal practice areas, including commercial transactions, bankruptcy, corporate law, employee benefits, estate plan-

ning and administration, finance and securities, food and drug regulation, environmental, local government, real estate and construction, tax, and trade regulation and antitrust.

WORLDWIDE LEGAL NETWORK

Being the best is the objective of Chambliss, Bahner & Stophel. In addition to its staff of attorneys, paralegals, and support personnel based in Chattanooga, the firm is proud to be a member of Commercial Law Affiliates (CLA), a worldwide organization of high-quality, independent business, tax, and litigation law firms. CLA consists of more than 220 law firms with nearly 5,000 attorneys covering the United States (excluding Iowa) and more

CHAMBLISS, BAHNER & STOPHEL'S OFFICES ARE LOCATED IN THE CENTRAL BUSINESS DISTRICT OF DOWNTOWN CHATTANOOGA.

than 70 countries on six continents. This affiliation allows the firm to provide a breadth and depth of service not available through any other Chattanooga firm.

STRAIGHTFORWARD APPROACH

Chambliss, Bahner & Stophel understands that clients need to have their legal work handled promptly and at a cost proportional to its importance. The firm's approach to the practice of law is, therefore, simple and straightforward. Its attorneys listen carefully to what clients want to accomplish and work closely with them to achieve their objectives. To control costs, the firm focuses on essential points and discourages negotiations and litigation over unimportant issues. Further, the firm typically limits the number of lawyers working on a matter to increase efficiency and reduce client expense. Yet, when necessary, Chambliss, Bahner & Stophel has the breadth, size, and resources to handle very large projects facing immediate deadlines.

Chambliss, Bahner & Stophel delivers results that are timely, cost effective, and practical. Recognizing that clients face an increasingly competitive business environment, the firm practices law with an eye toward results where they count most—on the client's bottom line.

The firm encourages its lawyers to draw on the resources of every staff member. Accordingly, each client can receive the benefit of the firm's collective experience and knowledge.

The firm is also committed to taking advantage of technological tools that broaden its capabilities, help contain costs, and provide better service to clients. To facilitate the client communication system, the firm incorporates state-of-the-art communication, including Internet access, voice mail, electronic mail, and the capacity to transmit and receive on-line documents via an integrated network.

PROFESSIONAL AND CIVIC COMMITMENT

The firm's lawyers are active participants in a wide variety of professional associations that have earned them numerous distinc-

ROBERT BOYER

ROBERT BOYER

tions and enhanced their legal expertise. Various members of the firm frequently are speakers and authors on topics within their fields of expertise. Several of the firm's lawyers have been recognized in *The Best Lawyers in America*, while others have held political offices or key positions in large corporations.

Virtually all of the firm's attorneys are active in civic and charitable organizations, serving in various leadership and advisory capacities.

In addition, Chambliss, Bahner & Stophel has striven continuously to be a good corporate citizen, having provided sponsorships, scholarships, and promotional assistance to numerous civic, cultural, educational, and charitable events and organizations.

Chambliss, Bahner & Stophel is a law firm whose tradition of excellence is matched only by its legacy of service—both for its clients and for its community.

FROM TOP:
THE FIRM HAS BEEN SIGNIFICANTLY INVOLVED IN THE REDEVELOPMENT OF CHATTANOOGA'S RIVERFRONT, REPRESENTING OWNERS, DEVELOPERS, AND FINANCIAL INSTITUTIONS.

FROM ITS BEGINNING IN 1886, CHAMBLISS, BAHNER & STOPHEL HAS MAINTAINED A TRADITION OF EXCELLENCE AND SERVICE TO ITS CLIENTS AND ITS COMMUNITY.

THE FIRM HANDLES A BROAD ARRAY OF LITIGATION FOR CLIENTS THROUGHOUT THE REGION AND NATIONALLY.

BRUCE C. BAILEY IS CERTIFIED AS A BUSINESS BANKRUPTCY SPECIALIST AND DANA B. PERRY IS CERTIFIED AS AN ELDER LAW SPECIALIST. CERTIFICATION AS PATENT, INTELLECTUAL PROPERTY, HEALTH CARE, LABOR AND EMPLOYMENT, BUSINESS PLANNING, ACQUISITIONS, COMMERCIAL TRANSACTIONS, CORPORATE LAW, EMPLOYEE BENEFITS, ADMINISTRATION, FINANCE AND SECURITIES, FOOD AND DRUG REGULATION, ENVIRONMENTAL, LOCAL GOVERNMENT, REAL ESTATE, CONSTRUCTION, TAX, TRADE REGULATION AND ANTITRUST SPECIALIST NOT CURRENTLY AVAILABLE IN TENNESSEE. NO ATTORNEYS ARE CERTIFIED AS CIVIL TRIAL, CRIMINAL TRIAL, CONSUMER BANKRUPTCY, CREDITOR'S RIGHTS, ACCOUNTING MALPRACTICE, LEGAL MALPRACTICE, MEDICAL MALPRACTICE, AND ESTATE PLANNING SPECIALIST BY THE TENNESSEE COMMISSION ON CONTINUING LEGAL EDUCATION AND SPECIALIZATION.

ROBERT BOYER

Connecticut General Life Insurance Company,
a CIGNA HealthCare Company

ONNECTICUT GENERAL LIFE INSURANCE COMPANY, A CIGNA HealthCare Company, is new to the Chattanooga area in name only. Its local ancestry can be traced to 1887, when Provident Life and Accident was established in the area. In 1995, Provident sold its group medical insurance business to Healthsource, Inc., which, in turn, was bought by CIGNA Corporation in 1997. With the completion of that

purchase, Healthsource Provident Administrators, Inc. officially became part of Connecticut General Life Insurance Company in 1998 and joined the CIGNA HealthCare family—one of America's leading group health plan insurers and administrators.

The Chattanooga operation is the third-largest CIGNA HealthCare employer outside its Bloomfield, Connecticut, headquarters. This major local presence serves as an operating base for three important CIGNA HealthCare initiatives: a national accounts team, the firm's new preferred provider organization (PPO) product, and a service center, which houses a Medicare unit, an imaging facility, two claims payment units, and a service administrator supporting a major portion of the company's health maintenance organization (HMO) subsidiaries.

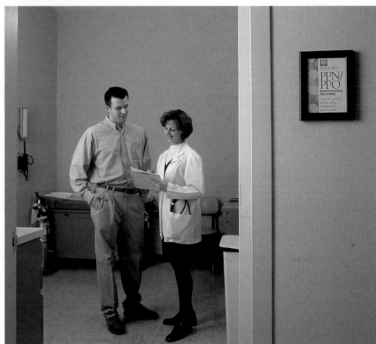

SERVING LARGE, NATIONAL ACCOUNTS

CIGNA HealthCare is a major player in the national accounts arena—a business segment that includes the largest organizations in the nation with 5,000 or more em-

ployees, often at various locations. Ranking among the top three competitors in that market, CIGNA HealthCare enjoys a number of advantages that are particularly attractive to national accounts. The company is known for its account management competency, long-term stability, national medical management competency, and cost performance, as well as the depth and breadth of its managed care networks and products.

According to James H. Pesnell, senior vice president of national accounts, "Our team here in Chattanooga has a long history of providing the responsive service and experienced account management that major companies require. Couple that background with CIGNA HealthCare's strong medical management capabilities and extensive provider networks, and the advantages we offer these types of customers become readily apparent."

The company's nationwide provider network contracts with some 3,500 hospitals and more than 205,000 credentialed physicians and specialists. Furthermore, CIGNA HealthCare

offers a full portfolio of health care plans that offer medical, dental, pharmaceutical, vision, and behavioral coverages—most of which are available in a variety of cost-effective health care solutions, ranging from managed indemnity plans and PPOs to wellness-focused HMOs and point-of-service plans. The firm can use its diverse array of plan designs, options, and funding alternatives to tailor a solution for virtually any group, in any location, nationwide.

Such broad access to medical care and responsive health care solutions accounts, in part, for CIGNA HealthCare's impressive membership totals. The company currently serves more than 15 million people nationwide with medical, dental, and mental health coverages.

But other factors contribute to CIGNA HealthCare's popularity, which goes beyond a prominence with national accounts to include its capabilities with companies having as few as 50 employees. Most notably, CIGNA HealthCare has a point of view that is unique for a national health care company: It believes that the delivery of health care should be

CIGNA HEALTHCARE OFFERS A WIDE PORTFOLIO OF HEALTH PLANS AND OTHER EMPLOYEE BENEFITS TO ITS CUSTOMERS. THE FIRM CAN USE ITS BROAD ARRAY OF PLAN DESIGNS, OPTIONS, AND FUNDING ALTERNATIVES TO TAILOR A SOLUTION FOR VIRTUALLY ANY GROUP, IN ANY LOCATION, NATIONWIDE (TOP).

SOPHISTICATED SCANNING EQUIPMENT AND HIGHLY ADVANCED COMPUTER SYSTEMS HELP CIGNA HEALTHCARE PRODUCE FAST, ACCURATE CLAIMS PAYMENTS (BOTTOM).

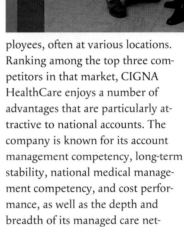

determined by local needs. Accordingly, the firm's medical decision-making processes are physician led and patient focused, and decisions are reached in the community being served—not from afar. As a result, CIGNA HealthCare's products and programs support close, reassuring physician-patient relationships.

A New PPO Product

Another vein of CIGNA Health-Care's Chattanooga-based expertise is being tapped to create its newest health care solution: a PPO product that offers customers access to CIGNA HealthCare's national network portfolio of PPOs, which is being consolidated to include networks associated with the recently acquired Healthsource-Provident Administrators, Inc. The Chattanooga team is well suited to manage this effort, having years of experience identifying, building, and managing PPO network solutions on a market-by-market basis.

The new product will offer customers an extensive mix of owned, leased, and customer-arranged networks, contracted at competitive rates. Customers will also benefit from responsive health information services, two levels of medical management, and optional services focused on keeping employees healthy. The new PPO product is forecast to experience rapid growth and be a major contributor to the firm's continued efforts with national accounts.

The Hamilton Village Service Center

Employing about half of CIGNA HealthCare's Chattanooga-area employees, the service center at Hamilton Village is home to operating units supporting Medicare, PPO, and point-of-service medical claims, as well as dental claims. The facility also houses the Regional Operations Center (ROC), which provides claims and administrative services to several CIGNA HealthCare operations, including HMO plans in Tennessee, Georgia, Texas, Arkansas, and Kentucky. The ROC processes claim payments, handles most enrollment and billing activities, and supports a variety of member services, provider relations, and medical management initiatives. The unit also has its own

financial area, which handles accounts payable and financial reporting requirements, and its own human resource personnel, who help keep the facility staffed with well-trained and responsive employees.

Giving Back to the Community

In both national and local arenas, CIGNA HealthCare is committed to charitable giving and employee involvement. Locally, the firm has actively supported—through contributions and employee volunteers—such programs as Relay for Life

(advancing the fight against cancer) and Walktoberfest (benefiting efforts to control diabetes). Other local support includes sponsorship of the fireworks display at the Riverbend Festival, Chattanooga's 10-day music event held each summer. Nationally, the company is a major contributor to the March of Dimes.

With its firm grounding in Chattanooga and a clear commitment to its customers and the communities in which it operates, CIGNA HealthCare is poised to maintain and enhance its hard-earned position on the national health care horizon.

CIGNA HealthCare service representatives have the knowledge and training to answer customer questions courteously and expertly (top).

CIGNA's commitment to promoting the health of its members has been nationally recognized. Wellness programs for expectant mothers are just one example of how CIGNA puts its slogan—"a business of caring"—into action (bottom).

Provident Companies, Inc.

THROUGH MORE THAN A CENTURY OF ECONOMIC AND SOCIAL CHANGE, Provident has been providing clients with disability income insurance. Today, Provident Companies, Inc. is North America's leader in disability insurance, with $1.7 billion of individual and group long-term disability premiums in force. Recognized for leadership in product design, claims handling, and service for customers, Provident is committed to reaching and serving growing numbers of customers in the individual and employee benefit markets.

Provident currently serves its individual insurance customers by providing product choices to meet disability income insurance and related financial protection needs. For its corporate customers, Provident provides a complete portfolio of disability, life, and specialty employee benefits with flexible financing options that enable employers to offer highly competitive benefits at an affordable cost.

Originally known as the Mutual Medical Aid and Accident Insurance Company, Provident offered accident and sickness insurance to high-risk workers who ran the blast furnaces, mines, and lumber camps of Tennessee and the surrounding areas. Today, the company employs some

PROVIDENT IS THE LARGEST DISABILITY INSURER IN NORTH AMERICA, AND THE COMPANY'S EMPLOYEES SHARE A COMMON COMMITMENT TO BUILDING BUSINESS THROUGH EXCELLENCE IN DISABILITY PRODUCT DESIGN, CLAIMS HANDLING, AND CUSTOMER SERVICE.

5,500 people worldwide and 2,300 in the Chattanooga area.

A Focus on Disability Insurance

In 1995, Provident sold its group medical business and began to exit the group pension business, with the purpose of sharpening the company's focus on both individual and group disability insurance, life coverages, nonmedical employee benefits, and voluntary benefits. Two years later, the company moved boldly to hone that focus even further: Provident bought the Paul Revere Corporation, one of the nation's largest disability insurers, and GENEX Services, Inc., a company highly regarded for its disability case management and vocational rehabilitation services.

"Provident is North America's leader in disability income insurance," says Thomas A.H. White, vice president of corporate relations. "We are building on our success by broadening product offerings to serve a wider range of customers, strengthening our commitment to help return people to work after a disability, and enhancing our service to make it easier to do business with us."

While the company's product line is strongly focused on disability insurance, the firm also offers other coverages, including life, accidental death and dismemberment, and cancer. Additionally, Provident offers dental coverage, underwritten by Ameritas Life Insurance Corporation, and immediate and deferred annuities, available through American General.

Provident distributes its products and services to two markets: individual customers and corporate customers. For individual customers, Provident markets individual disability income insurance and individual life insurance and annuities. Provident offers choices in disability income insurance that meet the specific needs of customers, recognizing differences in age, income, and life-style. Coverage choices include full or partial loss of the ability to earn an income and

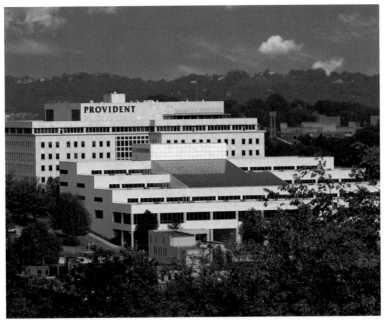

disability caused by accident, critical illness, and/or any injury or illness.

To complement its disability portfolio, Provident provides other protection-oriented insurance products to its individual customers. The company offers term, universal, and whole life insurance, as well as immediate and deferred annuities, to help customers build a complete financial protection plan.

Provident works with corporate customers and their advisers to design creative solutions to companies' employee benefits needs. By offering flexible, integrated products and funding options, Provident helps balance employer and employee benefit costs in competitive benefit plans.

A New Research Center

Within the context of its two prime markets, Provident always remains primarily focused on disability insurance. That point was underscored in December 1997, when Provident announced the formation of a Disability Research Alliance with the University of Tennessee at Chattanooga (UTC) to develop the Center for Disability Research, a downtown health, rehabilitation, and research complex. The center, slated for completion in 1999, will advance research, education, and clinical programs designed to prevent and reduce the impact of work disability. Such efforts fully complement Provident's own expertise in disability management

and emphasize the firm's commitment to be an innovator in that field.

While many companies may talk about return-to-work initiatives and managed disability, Provident has demonstrated an unparalleled commitment to this strategy. Managing disability is important because of its impact on employer payroll costs. Lost time in the workplace due to employee illness and injury represents a significant cost for employers today. Provident is committed to helping employees make adaptations and receive treatment so that they can resume productive and fulfilling lives through advancement of return-to-work programs, innovative claims management, and case management by a full complement of medical and rehabilitation specialists.

Provident's contribution to the community has laid the groundwork for an even stronger relationship with Chattanooga citizens. Among the many organizations and foundations actively and financially supported by the company are the United Way, local scholarship and Adopt-A-School programs, Kids on the Block, Arthritis Foundation, Junior Achievement, Allied Arts, and Chattanooga Symphony and Opera Association. These contributions, combined with successful business practices, firmly cement Provident as both a business and community leader in Chattanooga.

FEW COMPANIES IN THE WORLD CAN MATCH THE MANUFACTURING FEATS OF Chattanooga's ABB CE Power Products Manufacturing. The sheer size of the products ABB CE produces is amazing in itself. This premier maker of pressure parts for power-generating systems and other industries can "bend" a 50-ton, nine-inch-thick steel plate, and can fabricate steel drums weighing up to 350 tons and running up to 110 feet long.

Furthermore, all these products are formed to exacting specifications; delivered within an aggressive, customer-driven time frame; and made to withstand demanding metallurgical requirements.

These are impressive accomplishments for a firm whose roots can be traced to simple boiler making. ABB CE's Chattanooga presence dates to 1888 and the Walsh & Weidner Company, a boiler manufacturer, which merged in 1928 with Casey & Hedges Company, an ironworks. Combustion Engineering (CE) soon purchased that entity. In 1990, CE became a wholly owned subsidiary of ABB, a Switzerland-based manufacturer of power-generating systems.

Today, ABB CE employs about 600 people at its Chattanooga facility, where the company focuses on two main product lines—tubular and plate-formed products—which are used in steam-generating systems. Tubular products include superheater/reheater assemblies, panels, economizers, loose tubes, and chromized products. Among the assortment of plate products are steam drums, pressure vessels, package boiler assemblies, heavy wall fittings, and steel fabrication for the shipbuilding industry.

SERVICE DRIVEN, CUSTOMER FOCUSED

Until the mid-1980s, most of the firm's work involved building steam-generating systems for new power plants. The demand for new plants began to diminish around 1985, as the domestic utility industry began to respond to an overcapacity. That development, combined with increased environmental requirements and the more recent deregulation of the electrical utilities industry, shifted the bulk of ABB CE's business into aftermarket products and services. Today, nearly 75 percent of the firm's work is in retrofits—systems that increase the power-producing efficiency of an existing plant, reduce environmental risks, or update a plant's older components.

ABB CE has adapted well to the new marketplace realities. The firm has become a service-driven, customer-focused organization. With customers needing projects started and completed quicker than ever before, the company has dramatically reduced its cycle time. Furthermore, ABB CE now works with customers in a team environment, offering the services of technical personnel who help make sure finished products meet customer expectations. All ABB CE employees are encouraged to participate in procedural, manufacturing, and continuous-improvement processes.

The company has also successfully expanded into new products and markets. In the past, the Chattanooga facility built product for only ABB CE-designed plants. However, over the last several years, the company has built products for other original equipment manufacturers, accounting for 10 percent of the firm's workload. ABB CE has also diversified into the shipbuilding industry, providing fabricated steel products for commercial ships and offshore oil platforms.

Additionally, the company has invested some $25 million in new equipment. As a result, ABB CE is one of the most advanced pressure-part-fabricating facilities in the world and one of the world's largest power generation suppliers. This prominence is supported by the firm's engineering, metallurgical, and consulting services. ABB CE's metallurgical laboratory, for example, helps maintain the technical superiority of the company's own manufacturing operation and provides critical technical help to customers.

Teamed with ABB's other subsidiaries and their far-reaching manufacturing capabilities, ABB CE offers Chattanooga customers a complete power generation solution. Or, as the folks at ABB CE like to say, "from the coal pile to the light switch, we do it all."

ABB CE POWER PRODUCTS MANUFACTURING'S FACILITY IS LOCATED ON THE TENNESSEE RIVER BENEATH LOOKOUT MOUNTAIN.

GREAT CUSTOMER SERVICE HAS TRADITIONALLY BEEN A HALLMARK of successful companies. Indeed, when the South Chattanooga Savings Bank opened in 1889, it won—and then kept—customers by going the extra mile for its patrons. The bank's long-standing tradition of customer-first thinking powered the firm's growth throughout this century as it expanded and evolved into Hamilton National Bank and then First Tennessee Bank.

CREATING VALUE

Today's competitive environment, however, demands more than great customer service. That's why First Tennessee has turned to a more vigorous challenge to guide its growth: to create value for its constituents and build loyalty—one opportunity at a time.

First Tennessee relies on a concept called Firstpower: a companywide culture that encourages the organization to stay focused on those attributes that build value. Firstpower has been the driving force behind a number of initiatives that have made a lasting, positive impact at First Tennessee. For example, the bank has received some of the highest marks in the industry related to customer and employee retention. It was given top honors by *Business Week* magazine as one of the most family-friendly companies in America. And First Tennessee has produced a financial record that is the envy of bank holding companies throughout America.

Such strong determination to add value has led the bank to describe itself with an equally bold tag line: All Things Financial. First Tennessee National Corporation, the parent company of First Tennessee Bank, can supply ample evidence to back that claim. Recently, for example, about half of the firm's revenues have come from national business lines: mortgage banking, capital markets, transaction processing, and, to a growing extent, consumer finance, investment management, and insurance. These lines of business, alongside the company's traditional strength in regional retail/commercial banking, indicate that it has the huge breadth of services needed to deliver on its slogan.

BANKING, INVESTMENT, AND INSURANCE SERVICES

First Tennessee ranks number one in the state in deposit and loan market share, and has the number one deposit market share in four of the state's major metropolitan markets, including southeastern Tennessee.

Locally, First Tennessee has 21 branch locations offering a complete array of retail and commercial banking products and services. These offerings include a variety of checking and savings account options, products that give businesses tighter control of their finances, and on-line banking applications. The business-oriented products include services that help businesses manage tax payments more efficiently, increase their control over cash flow, and transact banking via computer. First Tennessee's on-line banking capabilities are among the most advanced in the nation, anchored by FTB Online—the first Java-enabled suite of Internet banking, financial analysis, and planning applications for customers.

First Tennessee also offers investment services that help customers evaluate financial goals and select from a wide assortment of investment products. Additionally, First Tennessee is a growing force in the insurance business, offering ways to protect automotive and home investments, and family finances in the event of a death.

With its portfolio of financial products and emphasis on adding value, First Tennessee's second century promises all the Firstpower needed to continue the success that has greeted it since opening its doors more than 100 years ago.

STELLA ANDERSON, SENIOR VICE PRESIDENT AND MANAGER OF THE PERSONAL TRUST DIVISION FOR FIRST TENNESSEE BANK, DISCUSSES TRUST INVESTMENT MANAGEMENT WITH FORT JONES, ONE OF THE BANK'S PERSONAL TRUST OFFICERS (LEFT).

THE EXECUTIVE MANAGEMENT OF FIRST TENNESSEE BANK IS DETERMINED TO CREATE VALUE FOR ITS CONSTITUENTS AND BUILD LOYALTY—ONE OPPORTUNITY AT A TIME (RIGHT).

RICK OWENS PHOTOGRAPHY

URING THE 19TH CENTURY, BARONESS MATHILDE D'ERLANGER AND her husband, Baron Fredric Emile d'Erlanger, were well known for their contributions to the betterment of society. When they donated the original $5,000 to fund a hospital in Chattanooga, however, little did they realize that their generosity would give birth to an institution whose own acts of caring would span more than a century.

Since its founding in 1891, Erlanger Health System (EHS) has grown steadily to become the largest public hospital in Tennessee and one of America's leading medical centers. Serving the citizens of southeast Tennessee, north Georgia, north Alabama, the western Carolinas, and southeast Kentucky, EHS is the only system in the 200-mile-wide region with the resources to provide all of the health care services needed by area residents.

ERLANGER MEDICAL CENTER: THE CORNERSTONE

Anchoring EHS is Erlanger Medical Center (EMC), located near downtown Chattanooga. Each year, more than 250,000 people pass through the medical center's doors. EMC offers the most diverse scope of services found anywhere in the area, and this diversity greatly contributes to the high level of quality care for which the facility is noted. Physicians have the ability to call on a variety of areas of expertise, and have a wide array of the most technologically advanced resources at their disposal.

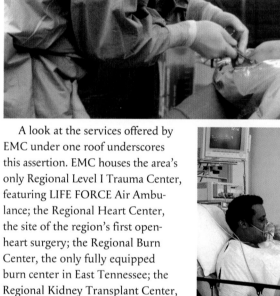

A look at the services offered by EMC under one roof underscores this assertion. EMC houses the area's only Regional Level I Trauma Center, featuring LIFE FORCE Air Ambulance; the Regional Heart Center, the site of the region's first open-heart surgery; the Regional Burn Center, the only fully equipped burn center in East Tennessee; the Regional Kidney Transplant Center, the only organ transplant service in the region; and the Tennessee Craniofacial Center, widely recognized as one of the finest facial reconstructive centers in the country.

In addition to these exclusive services, EMC offers other centers of excellence. These include the Regional Women's Center, the Regional Cancer Center, and the Southeastern Hand Institute. Erlanger's main campus also includes the region's largest intensive care system and state-of-the-art surgery facilities.

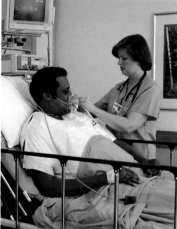

growth, continually adjusting its range of services and specialties to maintain the high level of care for which it is noted. One factor, though, has remained the same: It is the only area hospital specially designed to serve children. With more than 40 pediatric specialties available 24 hours a day and an emergency room that only serves kids, T.C. Thompson Children's Hospital continues its long tradition of meeting the health care needs of all children in the region.

Children's Hospital is joined by several other specialty and primary care facilities that are part of EHS. Among them are Erlanger East, a

DEDICATION TO CHILDREN'S WELL-BEING

T.C. Thompson Children's Hospital heads the list of other facilities that are part of EHS. Originally dedicated in July 1928, this hospital has seen years of transformation and

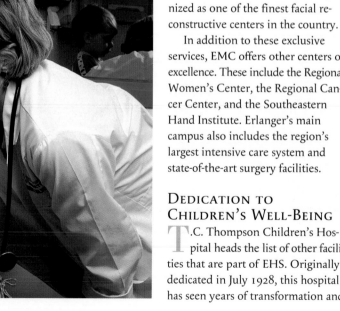

state-of-the-art primary care and out-patient surgery campus; Erlanger North, a full-service community hospital serving residents north of the Tennessee River; Miller Eye Center, a national center of excellence and the first hospital in Tennessee dedicated to eye care; Women's East Pavilion, a modern birth and gynecological facility attached to Erlanger East; the Alton Park-Dodson Avenue Community Health Centers and Westside Medical Home, three facilities providing a wide range of primary care services; and Contin-U-Care, a leader in innovative home health services.

EHS has invested significantly in broadening and unifying its health care offerings. For example, the new Medical Mall houses all outpatient services in one place, a 313,000-square-foot facility that is physically linked to the medical center and its parking garage. And the new Chattanooga LifeStyle Center, a partnership with the Sports Barn, Inc., is a 108,000-square-foot complex that unites a fitness center with sports

medicine services, an orthopedic treatment center, rehabilitation services, wellness programs, and nontraditional therapies, as well as learning and research centers.

COST-MANAGEMENT INITIATIVES

The goal of EHS is a healthier population able to access quality, comprehensive health care services at a low cost.

EHS is part of the Galaxy Health Alliance, which consists of 14 hospitals that have partnered to provide a cohesive health care delivery system for the 1 million people in its service areas. By working together, the hospitals in the alliance can reduce the cost of health care by ensuring that patients are treated at the right place and at the right time.

A HISTORY OF GIVING

The EHS mission is to provide all patients with excellent care, regardless of their ability to pay. Annually, EHS spends more than $20 million on free care to area

citizens. In addition, the staff of Erlanger volunteers thousands of hours in civic duty. For more than a century, EHS has continued to fulfill the vision of Baron and Baroness d'Erlanger.

NAME A UNIVERSITY IN TENNESSEE THAT HAS A TOURING ORCHESTRA, an antidrug gymnastic team, a wellness program for students and employees, and . . . a dollhouse? ✳ The unique answer among Tennessee's 35 private colleges is Southern Adventist University (SAU), just east of Chattanooga in the small city of Collegedale. ✳ From humble beginnings as the Graysville School in 1892, SAU

has become a nationally recognized and accredited institution of higher education. In 1916, the expanding school relocated 30 miles south across the Tennessee River to Jim Thatcher's farmland. This purchase included his daughter's playhouse. The tiny building served an astonishing number of purposes in the early years and still intrigues campus visitors. The area was named Collegedale in anticipation of a growing college community.

And grow it did. The junior college became a senior college—Southern Missionary College—in 1944. To more clearly identify itself as a liberal arts institution, in 1982, the college again changed its name, this time to Southern College of Seventh-day Adventists. Finally, in 1996, the most dramatic change occurred: the school began to offer graduate programs, and Southern Adventist University was born.

Today, the university has a student body of about 1,700. Its 1,000 acres are cradled between the forested slopes of White Oak Mountain

SPRING BLOSSOMS ON SOUTHERN ADVENTIST UNIVERSITY'S 1,000-ACRE CAMPUS FRAME WRIGHT HALL, THE ADMINISTRATION BUILDING, TO PERFECTION (TOP).

THE PROMENADE IS MORE THAN A WALKWAY FROM CLASS TO CLASS. IT'S A PLACE TO STUDY OR TALK WITH FRIENDS (BOTTOM).

and Bauxite Ridge. Two residence halls flank the administration building and house 65 percent of the students. The university operates a classical-music-format public radio station (FM90.5 WSMC), a book and gift store, a printing facility, and the largest health food store in the Southeast.

Recognizing a connection between healthful living and effective learning, SAU students enjoy the benefits of a gymnasium, track,

swimming pool, and tennis courts, as well as vegetarian fare in the campus cafeteria and snack shops. In 1995, SAU's employee wellness program earned it one of the first gold-level Well Workplace awards in the state. Student leaders conduct their own Partners at Wellness program. Corporate/community wellness management is among SAU's 40 baccalaureate majors. SAU's Gym-Masters put on electrifying shows at NBA and NCAA halftimes and at assembly programs with an antidrug message for elementary and high school students.

EXPANDING THE CORE MISSION

As SAU positions itself for 21st-century growth, administrators are committed to the university's core mission of providing education integrated with Christian values. One of 87 globe-spanning colleges and universities operated by the Seventh-day Adventist Church, SAU emphasizes the growth and education of the whole student. SAU does not discriminate in admissions on the basis of age, gender, race, color, ethnic or national origin, religion, or handicap. "I highly value caring about people, and communication," says SAU President Dr. Gordon Bietz. "I also value an intelligent faith."

Such concern and openness have spurred tremendous growth. In 1998, SAU enjoyed increased enrollment, with students from 46 states and 55 countries. Minority enrollment increased among almost every ethnic group.

A University Offering Diversity

Academically speaking, SAU offers 40 undergraduate majors, five graduate degree programs, 20 associate degree majors, and certification in auto body and auto mechanics. The university's nursing and elementary education programs are particularly strong, and are recognized by the National League for Nursing and the National Council for the Accreditation of Teacher Education, respectively. SAU's medium-sized campus is home to one of the largest "ladder" (associate's and bachelor's degrees in science) nursing programs in Tennessee.

The 21st Century Classroom and Teaching Materials Center, resources in the School of Education, are well known even beyond Chattanooga. Preprofessional programs include several health fields and engineering. The business, psychology, and religion majors are popular, and draw students from all over the globe.

As testimony to the education it provides, Southern has a strong acceptance record into medical, dental, and law schools. Internships for computer science students have placed them with AT&T for work on a voice recognition system and with NASA to upgrade ground control for the Hubble space telescope. Southern's physics department, though small, has gained international attention for its teacher/student scientific research leading to a periodic chart of molecules.

Graduate programs include master's degrees in business administration, counseling, education, religion, and software engineering. Unique classes have capitalized on Southern's location, such as a field biology class that explores Smoky Mountain plant life and a Civil War class in which students take on personae of mid-19th-century Americans to actually "live" history.

Southern administers an overseas volunteer service program that includes teaching English to students

in Pacific Rim and other countries. A colleges abroad program gives students the option of a year of study in Argentina, Austria, France, or Spain. Southern has business education affiliations with colleges in Orlando and South Africa, and an affiliation for marine biology courses on the Washington coast. The bachelor of science degree in nursing is offered at three sites in Florida.

Giving Back to Chattanooga

Giving back to the community has always been an important part of life at SAU. Faculty and students are active as community volunteers. In addition, for several years, an entire day has taken these volunteers from the classroom into the community for service.

Throughout the calendar year, SAU offers a rich variety of lectures and concerts that are well attended by the surrounding community. The Eugene A. Anderson Heiller Organ Concert Series (held in the Collegedale Seventh-day Adventist Church on campus) and the Chamber Music Series bring world-class musicians and ensembles to play for students, faculty, and the community. Performances by Southern's own music ensembles—including an 80-piece orchestra, a large concert band, and several choral groups—draw listeners to the campus.

Other popular events include the E.A. Anderson Lecture Series in Business, the Florence Oliver Anderson Lecture Series in Nursing, and the E.O. Grundset Lecture Series in Biology. The new venue for the latter is Southern's Hickman Science Center, dedicated in 1997. A conference center hosts overnight guests and groups such as Elderhostel students.

As Southern Adventist University builds on the strength of its Christian foundation and opens new doors into the 21st century, its ministry to the needs of students—both young and old, and from Chattanooga to the Czech Republic to China—remains a constant amid dynamic change.

STUDENTS OF BIOLOGY AND THE OTHER SCIENCES ENJOY THE UP-TO-DATE LABORATORY FACILITIES IN THE HICKMAN SCIENCE CENTER, COMPLETED IN 1997.

THE 21ST CENTURY CLASSROOM TEACHES FUTURE TEACHERS HOW TO USE COMPUTERS AND EDUCATIONAL SOFTWARE IN THE SCHOOL ENVIRONMENT.

American Manufacturing Company

THE STORY OF AMERICAN MANUFACTURING COMPANY IS ONE OF A century-old Chattanooga business built upon the principles of character, quality, and service. In 1898, a former Union officer from Indiana named William Weber and his son-in-law, James B. Robinson, acquired what was then the Chattanooga Buckle Company. Originally located on the corner of Chestnut and Water streets downtown, American began as a primary producer of hardware vital to the harness and saddlery trade.

Soon after the turn of the century, the company branched out to produce other industrial products, including shelves for some of the earliest stoves and ranges made in the country, followed by a line of wire floral goods such as easels, wreaths, plant stands, and hanging baskets. Around the 1930s, prompted by the advent of bottled, carbonated beverages originating in Chattanooga, American entered the merchandise display business, and quickly assumed a leadership position as a primary supplier of merchandise displays to the Coca-Cola Company and other leading beverage companies.

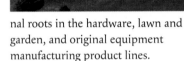

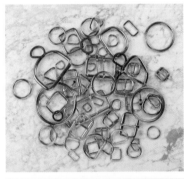

CHANGING WITH THE TIMES

Those early experiences in the display and store fixture industry began an evolution that continues to gain momentum as American approaches its second century in business. Over the past two decades, merchandising display has grown from the company's smallest to its largest product line. Though point-of-purchase displays now represent more than 75 percent of sales, American has maintained much of its origi-

nal roots in the hardware, lawn and garden, and original equipment manufacturing product lines.

American's primary emphasis is on the custom design and fabrication of products made of steel wire, tubing, sheet metal, and wood, along with signage and components of paper, plastics, and other materials. American has uniquely positioned itself as a prime manufacturer that also offers the creative and development services usually associated only with design houses. Its ability to produce large, complex display programs and offer customized warehousing and shipping services has placed American in the elite group of manufacturers qualified to handle national rollouts.

"There's no magic formula to our success, just a commitment to service that people have grown to expect. We don't sell to people, we

serve them," says Bill Hewgley, executive vice president of sales and marketing for American. "We are long-term players looking to build long-term relationships with our customers."

In 1993, Everett Warren of Nashville acquired American Manufacturing Company from the namesake and grandson of one of the founders, James B. Robinson of Chattanooga. Since that time, the company has realized significant growth and multiple expansions to accommodate sales growth. Today, American employs more than 200 people at its home office and 400,000-square-foot metal facility located on North Hawthorne Street in Chattanooga, and its 60,000-square-foot hardboard and wood fabrication plant in Decatur, Tennessee. Because of its reputation for creativity, quality, and service, American has developed a diverse portfolio of nationally recognized clients that includes McKee Foods, NK Lawn & Garden, Target, Wal-Mart, Eveready Battery, Keebler Foods, Service Merchandise, and Hershey's.

American Manufacturing Company and its employees are proud of the company's 100-year tradition of excellence and are prepared to enter the next century firmly committed to traditional American values.

W

HILE MANY PEOPLE MIGHT THINK THE USE OF RECYCLED PAPER IS a relatively recent development, the history of Rock-Tenn Company reveals quite a different story. Incorporated in Chattanooga in June 1918, Tennessee Paper Mills, Inc.—as the firm was then called—became the South's first recycled paperboard mill. ✳ John Stagmaier and A.M. Tomlinson founded the company to produce paperboard for the growing needs of box manufacturers in the South. Initially, they had planned to make straw board, then a widely used set-up grade board made from wheat straw. However, the two men turned to wastepaper as their primary source of raw material because wheat straw was harder to obtain and cost more to ship on its journey to the Chattanooga plant.

The idea of using wastepaper made good economic sense and proved fortuitous. By changing the raw material, Stagmaier and Tomlinson also changed the ultimate use of the board they manufactured, a change that addressed new developments in the packaging industry. Folding cartons were becoming increasingly popular as the packaging industry's primary component, replacing rigid setup boxes that had been commonly used up to that point. The recycled paperboard that Stagmaier and Tomlinson planned to produce was the ideal material to meet those emerging needs.

MILL DIVISION MEETS GROWING DEMAND

Through years of growth and several mergers, the original idea the founders conceived in 1917 has continued to pay off handsomely. In fact, Rock-Tenn's Mill Division truly seems to have the right product at the right time. Consumer goods manufacturers and retailers throughout the nation have found that using recycled paperboard helps them meet the increasing consumer demand for environmentally sound packaging. In recent years, use of recycled paperboard has grown at almost twice the rate of virgin substrates. The Mill Division's consumption of recovered paper prevents more than 380,000 tons from entering the nation's solid waste stream each year.

The Mill Division produces all grades of recycled paperboard and ships throughout the United States to paperboard converters, including Rock-Tenn's own Folding Carton and Partition Division. An ongoing modernization program has helped keep the Mill Division one of the most efficient manufacturers in the nation, producing the highest quality paperboard to meet customers' demanding graphic and structural design requirements.

The Mill Division is one of seven Rock-Tenn Company divisions. Headquartered in Norcross, Georgia, Rock-Tenn Company is a vertically integrated packaging company whose divisions produce everything from folding cartons to corrugated boxes to plastic packaging. The publicly held firm has upwards of 70 manufacturing facilities, and in 1997, acquired the Waldorf Corporation.

Despite its growth, the company has never lost sight of its commitment to its customers. The Mill Division, for example, has earned a long-standing reputation for superior service and quality, as well as prompt delivery. Remarkably, the Mill Division has retained some customers for more than 50 years.

By offering recycled paperboard as an effective alternative, Rock-Tenn's Mill Division proves that building a better mousetrap is not always the answer. Sometimes, it makes more sense to simply build the mousetrap out of better materials.

CLOCKWISE FROM TOP:
ROCK-TENN COMPANY'S CHATTANOOGA MILL HAS BEEN IN THIS LOCATION FOR MORE THAN 80 YEARS.

ROCK-TENN'S CARTON DIVISION MANUFACTURES A VARIETY OF PRODUCTS.

SORTING AND GRADING WASTE PAPER IS THE PRIMARY FUNCTION OF ROCK-TENN'S RECYCLED DIVISION.

E MIL J. BRACH FIRST BEGAN MAKING FRESH, CREAMY CARAMELS IN 1904, drawing crowds into his little "palace of sweets" in Chicago to taste his unique candies. Coincidentally, two years later, William E. Brock turned his eye toward handmade penny candies, hoping his business of making peanut brittle, fudge, and other confections would satisfy Chattanooga's sweet tooth. Each family-owned company worked hard to create a new palette of tasty treats, continually improve quality, and satisfy the ever growing demand. Both companies, as a result, became leading candy makers and household names.

A SMOOTH TRANSITION

Today, following an acquisition, the two companies form Brach & Brock Confections. With corporate headquarters in Chattanooga, the company now makes fresh candy in five locations, including the world's largest candy factory: a 2.3 million-square-foot plant in Chicago. Brach & Brock continues to thrive on the same family-driven energy, producing a large variety of tasty and delightful candies, including Milk Maid® caramels, Andes® mints, StarBrites® peppermints, and a full array of fruit snacks.

In 1994, Brach & Brock Confections became the fourth-largest candy company in the United States. New products and new marketing strategies are constantly being tested with an eye toward bringing the consumer the most flavorful, high-quality candies—all made with the best ingredients possible. Not surprisingly, the company now produces more than 400 million pounds of candy a year.

THE FRESH CANDY SHOPPE™

Who wants candy? The whole family! And chances are Mom, Dad, and the kids all crave something different. Brach & Brock has known that fact for a long time. The company's well-known Pick-A-Mix® bulk candy concept, a grocery favorite since 1958, has helped make Brach & Brock the dominant market share leader in loose candy—a concept the company pioneered.

Brach & Brock candies have long been mainstays of the candy aisle in the nation's supermarkets, but the company recognizes that supermarkets are changing. The new growth areas are emerging in high-image, perimeter sections such as floral, coffee, and bulk candy shops. These areas offer fresh, customized products that attract the consumer with more individual choice than prepackaged products.

Brach & Brock's Fresh Candy Shoppe™ concept spent two years in research and development at a cost of more than $1 million. The Fresh Candy Shoppe™ updates and expands the concept of family sweets and weekly treats with emphasis on freshness and brand recognition. The key to the Fresh Candy Shoppe™ lies in marketing the old favorites next to the new and popular branded treats. Freshness Service™, the company's method of setup and delivery, allows the Fresh Candy Shoppe™ to be replenished frequently through direct store delivery to its Fresh-Lok Sealed Bins, which pro-

WITH CORPORATE HEADQUARTERS IN CHATTANOOGA, BRACH & BROCK NOW MAKES FRESH CANDY IN FIVE LOCATIONS ACROSS THE COUNTRY (TOP).

BRACH'S FRESH CANDY SHOPPE™ OFFERS A COMPLETE VARIETY OF FAVORITES TO SATISFY THE WHOLE FAMILY. CUSTOMERS CAN MIX AND MATCH THEIR OWN SELECTIONS AT LOCAL GROCERY STORES (BOTTOM).

vide automatic product rotation and guaranteed freshness.

Found in local supermarkets and superstores—and, in the future, a host of other locations, including theaters and convenience stores— the Fresh Candy Shoppe™ lets everyone pick what they want and as much as they want, whether it's Special Treasures® and gourmet blends of fine chocolates for Mom and Dad, or Gummi Squirms® and Smucker's® jelly beans for the kids.

BRACH & BROCK'S BRANDS HIT THE SWEET SPOT

B rach & Brock has a unique portfolio of products and brands that hit the sweet spot. Several Brach & Brock's brands have been around for nearly a century, such as Milk Maid® caramels, Andes®, and StarBrites®.

Additionally, Brach & Brock has introduced a full range of new products in recent years, including Special Treasures® international toffees and several co-brands like Hi-C® gummi fruits, Smucker's® jelly beans, and Almond Supremes made with real Blue Diamond® almonds.

In addition to successes in the candy aisle, Brach & Brock competes exceptionally well in the fruit snacks category. The attraction of well-known products like Hi-C®, Batman™, Godzilla™, and Donkey Kong®— all delivering taste and nutrition— makes snacking just plain fun. Recent introductions of Chiquita™ and Hot Wheels™ fruit snacks have made Brach & Brock the fastest-growing manufacturer of fruit snacks. The strategy is to increase grocery and

other venue sales while providing the highest-quality ingredients and consumer satisfaction.

Brimming with fresh candy of every shape, color, and flavor, Brach & Brock looks forward to exponential growth of its Fresh Candy Shoppe™, packaged, seasonal, and

fruit snack treats in the coming years. With its marketing and product innovation in the United States continuing to set standards for the industry, and with its growing exports to Canada, Mexico, South America, and elsewhere, Brach & Brock's future couldn't be sweeter.

TWO OF BRACH & BROCK'S MOST POPULAR CANDY CHARACTERS WAVE TO TRAVELERS PASSING BY THE COMPANY'S PLANT AND CORPORATE HEADQUARTERS ON HIGHWAY 153.

A TEAM OF DEDICATED AND CONSCIENTIOUS EMPLOYEES PLAY AN ESSENTIAL ROLE IN BRACH & BROCK'S SUCCESS IN THE LOCAL AND NATIONAL CONFECTIONERY MARKETS AS WELL AS AROUND THE WORLD.

SunTrust Bank, Chattanooga, N.A.

unTrust Bank, Chattanooga, N.A. is heir to a long history of innovation, success, and community involvement. The firm can trace its beginnings to 1912, when Harry Probasco and his son, Scott, founded the American Trust and Banking Company in Chattanooga. Based on the pioneering idea that the services of two types of lending institutions—a commercial bank and a trust company—could be offered through one entity, the new bank was a quick success. Within a year, it had accumulated deposits of $358,000, produced $401,000 in loans, and raised capital of $200,000.

A Strong Financial Partner

Today, SunTrust Bank, Chattanooga, N.A. has the distinction of being the largest financial institution in Chattanooga, with commercial assets of $1.47 billion at the end of 1997. Locally, the firm employs some 600 people in 37 offices serving southeast Tennessee and northwest Georgia. SunTrust Bank, Chattanooga, N.A., however, is part of an even larger organization: SunTrust Bank, Inc. Based in Atlanta, SunTrust Bank, Inc. is the 19th-largest bank holding company in the nation and one of the most solid financial institutions in the industry, with total assets of $58 billion. SunTrust is also one of the largest U.S. investment managers, successfully managing more than $60 billion in assets for investment customers. Among banking organizations, the firm is the 18th-largest manager of mutual fund assets, having more than $6.9 billion under management.

As a vital part of the fast-growing Southeast, SunTrust Bank, Inc. has more than 20,000 employees serving more than 2 million personal and business customers. The bank has more than 740 branch offices in Tennessee, Georgia, Alabama, and Florida. Additionally, SunTrust maintains a network of better than 950 automated teller machines (ATMs) throughout the four-state area.

Building Relationships

Though SunTrust's strength and size offer customers many advantages, the firm's decentralized structure is most critical to the bank's main customer focus: relationship banking. "Having strong relationships means knowing our customers well and partnering with them," says Robert J. Sudderth Jr., chairman and chief executive officer, SunTrust Bank, Chattanooga, N.A. "That's why our ability to make local decisions based on local needs is so important. By being close by and community-focused, we develop a thorough understanding of our customers' comprehensive financial needs. In offering the finest products and services to meet those needs, we become partners in our customers' success—which is always the most gratifying part of our work."

According to Sudderth, SunTrust's employees are the key to the solid, partnering relationships it enjoys with customers: "SunTrust's competitive advantage is its people. We carefully select the best people for

our team, invest in their development, and strive to provide them with ongoing challenges and advancement."

R. Alton Duke, president, seconds Sudderth's comments. "We invite everyone and anyone to meet and talk with our people," he says. "They'll convince even the most skeptical that SunTrust is an organization of rare quality, integrity, and commitment—the one that people feel most comfortable choosing as their partner in success."

COMPREHENSIVE PRODUCTS AND SERVICES

SunTrust serves both personal and business customers with a broad array of products and services. As Sudderth points out, "Being part of the SunTrust family of banks has greatly increased our ability to meet our customers' needs."

One of the bank's core strengths is the trust and investment business. SunTrust Chattanooga has one of the largest trust departments in the Southeast, with approximately $4.5 billion in trust assets at the end of 1997. In addition, the bank offers, through SunTrust Securities, Inc., several proprietary mutual fund products and annuities.

SunTrust has a long list of other areas of expertise, as well. The maintaining and transferring of wealth through estate planning and trusts is one example. Another is business banking—offering services to concerns of all sizes, from the smallest to the largest. Additionally, SunTrust's private banking function, conveniently located in two of the largest hospitals in the tristate area, has taken personal service in the medical com-

munity to a new level. SunTrust's residential lending area is the largest in the Chattanooga market, with offices in Chattanooga and Cleveland, Tennessee, and in Fort Oglethorpe and Dalton, Georgia.

CONVENIENCE AND INNOVATION

SunTrust offers a variety of convenient ways for consumers to do their banking. The firm provides 24-hour banking through a local network of 25 ATMs in Hamilton and Bradley counties, or at thousands of Honor and Cirrus ATMs around the world. Through a partnership with Winn-Dixie, SunTrust Chattanooga has opened eight in-store branches for full-service banking on weekdays, evenings, and weekends. With that

innovative service, SunTrust became the first bank in Chattanooga to have branches open on Sundays for added customer convenience.

SunTrust's TeleBank service allows customers to use any Touch-Tone phone to access current account information, apply for a loan, order checks, and much more. Customers can also manage their finances on-line any time they want with SunTrust's PC Banking for personal and business accounts. In addition, customers can access SunTrust's Web site at www.suntrust.com to learn more about the bank's products and services.

INVESTING IN THE COMMUNITY

SunTrust has committed the bank's human and financial resources to improving and aiding the Chattanooga community and surrounding areas. "We shall always fashion our strategies to reflect our visions for this community. Whatever it takes—money, time, effort, technology—we are dedicated to making Chattanooga a better place," says Sudderth.

With its continued dedication to building strong relationships with the people and communities it serves, SunTrust promises to enhance the legacy of innovation, success, and commitment started so many years ago by the Probasco family.

SUNTRUST BROKE WITH TRADITION BY OPENING EIGHT IN-STORE BRANCHES IN THE WINN-DIXIE GROCERY STORES. THIS INNOVATIVE DELIVERY SERVICE OFFERS CUSTOMERS FULL-SERVICE BANKING, SEVEN DAYS A WEEK.

SUNTRUST HAS SERVED THE NORTHGATE AREA SINCE 1971. TO ACCOMMODATE THIS FAST-GROWING AREA, A NEW, 4,400-SQUARE-FOOT FACILITY WAS BUILT IN 1995.

FOUNDED IN 1927 BY J.A. GLASCOCK AND GARDNER BRIGHT AS A Chattanooga-based residential real estate company, the Fletcher Bright Company has grown to become one of the largest full-line commercial real estate firms in the United States. Despite its growth, the firm continues to be a family-run company. After the Glascock-Bright partnership ended, Gardner Bright continued to operate the business

as the sole proprietor. Upon Gardner Bright's death in 1960, his son Fletcher took over the reins, eventually incorporating the business in 1968 as the Fletcher Bright Company.

The firm is still guided by Fletcher Bright, who is chairman of the board. He is joined by John M. Martin, vice chairman of the board and executive vice president of the firm since 1969. Martin oversees the residential real estate brokerage business of the Fletcher Bright Company.

Both men are assisted by a contingent of their offspring. George Bright serves as president of the company. Clifford G. Martin is executive vice president, responsible for sales and leasing. John G. Martin II serves as a vice president, concentrating on property management, sales, and leasing. And Garrison E. Martin is a vice president, with duties in property management, leasing, and commercial and residential sales.

A MAJOR COMMERCIAL REAL ESTATE PLAYER

The Fletcher Bright Company is involved in a wide range of commercial real estate activities, including property management, sales, development, and leasing. The firm employs 60 people at its Chattanooga headquarters and has another eight employees working at its Atlanta branch office. During the past 30 years, the company has developed, syndicated, sold, purchased, leased, and financed shopping centers throughout the Southeast. The firm currently manages approximately 135 shopping centers in 15 states—primarily in the Southeast— ranging in size from 25,000 to 350,000 square feet. Through years of experience and an ever growing depth of knowledge, the Fletcher Bright Company has come to be counted among the nation's top shopping center management firms.

Statistics compiled in the early 1990s by *Monitor*, a publication devoted to commercial real estate, bear out the firm's national prominence. For example, the Fletcher Bright Company was ranked the 38th-largest shopping center management firm, based on total gross leasable area for open and enclosed shopping centers in all states. Similarly, the company was the 39th-largest developer and was ranked 24th in acquisitions. The company came in 12th in open shopping center management, 21st in open shopping center development, and 15th in open shopping center acquisition.

The Fletcher Bright Company has been awarded the Accredited Management Organization (AMO) designation through the Institute of Real Estate Management (IREM). Holders of the AMO designation have met the IREM's standards in the areas of education, experience,

THROUGH YEARS OF EXPERIENCE AND AN EVER GROWING DEPTH OF KNOWLEDGE, THE FLETCHER BRIGHT COMPANY HAS COME TO BE COUNTED AMONG THE NATION'S TOP SHOPPING CENTER MANAGEMENT FIRMS.

The firm currently manages approximately 135 shopping centers in 15 states—primarily in the Southeast—ranging in size from 25,000 to 350,000 square feet.

integrity, and fiscal responsibility. AMOs are full-service management firms having a thorough understanding of the problems and profits that property ownership and management can produce. The Fletcher Bright Company has two certified property managers on staff in the Chattanooga office.

Additionally, the firm serves as a commercial mortgage banker and is a member of the Mortgage Bankers Association. It is also mortgage correspondent for a number of life insurance companies.

A Leader in Residential Real Estate

In terms of residential sales volume, the Fletcher Bright Company is the fourth-largest real estate firm in the Chattanooga area. The company has two local residential sales offices: the downtown office at Market Court and the North River office at Ashland Terrace. The firm employs a total of 36 real estate agents and brokers, licensed in Tennessee and Georgia. These experienced agents offer customers and clients outstanding professional service and in-depth knowledge of the Chattanooga real estate market. Furthermore, they base their service on the National Association of Realtors Code of Ethics. The Fletcher Bright Company is a member of the Chattanooga Association of Realtors, the Tennessee Association of Realtors, and the National Association of Realtors.

The firm offers residential real estate customers a number of advantages: personalized service, direct communication with agents, a national relocation service, the Multiple List-

ing Service, and a home warranty program.

Relocation services are provided by Genesis Relocation Services—the largest national independent relocation service in the nation. Genesis offers customers moving assistance, help with trailing spouse employment, and a preapproved mortgage through Chase Manhattan Mortgage and Fleet Mortgage Service (with no cost to the purchaser until closing). The Fletcher Bright Company also

participates in the computerized Multiple Listing Service offered by the Chattanooga Association of Realtors. This service gives potential buyers instant access to all residential listings in the Greater Chattanooga area.

An active and strong competitor in two vibrant markets—commercial and residential real estate—the Fletcher Bright Company promises to play an important role in Chattanooga and beyond for many years to come.

The Fletcher Bright Company is the fourth-largest real estate firm in the Chattanooga area. The firm offers residential real estate customers a number of advantages: personalized service, direct communication with agents, a national relocation service, the Multiple Listing Service, and a home warranty program.

Baker, Donelson, Bearman & Caldwell

THE CHATTANOOGA OFFICE OF BAKER, DONELSON, BEARMAN & Caldwell may be a prime example of why the firm has risen to national prominence. Led by longtime partners Thomas A. Caldwell, T.O. Helton, and Richard B. Gossett, the Chattanooga office, with its more than 70 employees, is committed to serving local, regional, and national clients; understanding their needs; and working closely with them to achieve the desired results.

Such commitment has been well rewarded. Baker, Donelson, Bearman & Caldwell, the largest law firm in Tennessee, was cited by the *National Law Journal* in 1995 as one of America's fastest-growing firms. And recently, *U.S. Business Litigation* named Baker, Donelson the 119th-largest law firm in America.

A LOCAL FOCUS

Baker, Donelson's beginnings in the Chattanooga area date to 1964 as the firm of Stophel, Caldwell & Heggie, which, in 1986, became Caldwell, Heggie & Helton. After a merger in 1993, the local firm became the Chattanooga office of Baker, Donelson, Bearman & Caldwell.

But while the name has undergone a few alterations, the fundamental philosophy guiding Baker, Donelson certainly has not. "Though much in the law and in our organizational structure has changed through the years," says Caldwell, "the principles on which we have built our practice have remained constant."

For Caldwell, whose practice experience dates to 1953, the key to the firm's day-to-day success will always remain anchored in estate planning. "Early in my career," he says, "I taught classes at night to life insurance agents who were aspiring to earn their CLU [chartered life underwriter] designation. Through that association and the subsequent experience I had advising people about their estates, I found that estate planning touched people's lives in many ways. Understanding that complexity and finding well-reasoned solutions are the common themes that unite our efforts and form the basic foundation of our practice here in Chattanooga."

With that fundamental strength in mind, Caldwell is quick to point out that Baker, Donelson offers clients even more services. "The reason we merged in 1992 was to better serve our clients. With the merger, we added significant strength in the areas of federal and international law and public policy."

WORLD-CLASS CAPABILITIES

Baker, Donelson maintains eight full-service offices, which are located in Memphis, Nashville, Chattanooga, Knoxville, and Huntsville, Tennessee; Tri-Cities TN/VA; Jackson, Mississippi; and Washington, D.C. Though the firm concentrates its practice in the Southeast, Baker, Donelson's client list includes significant representation nationally and internationally.

No other firm in the region has the level of experience across so many practice areas, from management of corporate matters and transactions, complex litigation, alternative dispute resolution, and international transactions to industry-specific multidisciplinary teams. Employing more than 500 people, including attorneys, advisers, paralegals, and support staff, Baker, Donelson's practice is divided into five major departments and 18 practice areas: bankruptcy and creditors' rights, commercial lending, communications, corporate, environmental and energy, ERISA and employee benefits, estate planning and probate, health law, intellectual property, international, labor and employment, litigation, mergers and acquisitions, public policy, real estate, securities, tax, and transportation.

With more than 220 attorneys and senior public policy advisers, the firm has a considerable pool of resources available to handle any matter, regardless of size, as well as the critical experience and leading-edge technology to manage and communicate effectively between all offices. This capability allows the firm's attorneys to tap into a large base of industry and legal experience to better serve their clients. Each matter is aggressively managed to ensure efficiency and to maintain costs.

The firm represents companies from a wide range of industries,

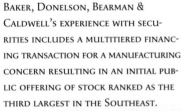

BAKER, DONELSON, BEARMAN & CALDWELL'S EXPERIENCE WITH SECURITIES INCLUDES A MULTITIERED FINANCING TRANSACTION FOR A MANUFACTURING CONCERN RESULTING IN AN INITIAL PUBLIC OFFERING OF STOCK RANKED AS THE THIRD LARGEST IN THE SOUTHEAST.

After Baker, Donelson's retention as statewide counsel, 17,000 pending product-liability asbestos cases were resolved in three months (TOP).

Before beginning construction on the world's largest Super Battery plant, one of the firm's clients needed environmental permits. To meet the client's deadlines, Baker, Donelson coordinated a fast-track process so that all permits were filed and in place within 60 days (BOTTOM).

including securities, technology, engineering, construction, telecommunications, restaurant chains and hospitality, insurance, banking, transportation, energy, defense, aerospace, consumer and commercial finance, investment banking, health care, pharmaceuticals, real estate development, and transportation. To stay abreast of industry-specific developments, the firm maintains in-house industry teams that explore issues and trends that will have an impact on clients in the future. In addition, Baker, Donelson actively recruits and trains the best new attorneys.

The following attorneys are certified as Civil Trial Specialists by the Tennessee Commission on Continuing Legal Education and Specialization: Thomas O. Helton (Chattanooga) and Jill M. Steinberg (Memphis). Randal S. Mashburn (Nashville) is certified as a Business Bankruptcy and Consumer Bankruptcy Specialist by the Tennessee Commission on Continuing Legal

Education and Specialization. Jerry Stauffer is Chair of the Litigation Department, which encompasses the areas of Employment, Environmental, Commercial Litigation, Tort, and Bankruptcy & Creditors' Rights. J. Porter Durham is Chair of the Corporate Department, which encompasses the areas of Intellectual Property, General Corporate/Mergers & Acquisitions, International, Public Policy, and Securities. Richard G. Cowart is Chair of the Health Law Department. Thomas L. Howard is Chair of the Tax Department. Robert C. Liddon is Chair of the Commercial Lending and Real Estate Department. These attorneys are not currently certified in any areas of Specialization.

COMMUNITY SERVICE

Baker, Donelson is committed to giving back to the community it serves. Each associate attorney donates 100 hours of service per year and/or pro bono work to civic, community, and charitable activities.

In Chattanooga, where the firm continues to actively support the arts and other charitable organizations, many of the associates have played roles in the city's renaissance. Caldwell, for example, has served the community in many capacities. He has been very active in the local Chamber of Commerce, the United Way campaign, and Orange Grove, a program that serves the community's developmentally disabled adults. The Orange Grove program, the largest of its kind in the nation, includes a recycling facility that helps reduce the city's landfill requirements while offering employment to citizens who might otherwise have a difficult time finding work. Caldwell's commitment to the success of Orange Grove has truly stood the test of time—he has been on the board of directors for 45 years.

Such commitment to the community, combined with a dedication to its ever growing client list, will continue to push Baker, Donelson, Bearman & Caldwell to the forefront of the legal field.

Certification as a Specialist in the following areas of practice by the Tennessee Commission on Continuing Legal Education and Specialization is not currently available: Environmental Law, Health Care Law, Labor & Employment Law, Patent, Trademark & Copyright Law, Securities Law, and Taxation Law. Certification as a Specialist in the following areas of practice by the Tennessee Commission on Continuing Legal Education and Specialization is currently available: Civil Trial, Business Bankruptcy, Consumer Bankruptcy, Creditors' Rights, and Estate Planning and Probate.

The Krystal Company

Founded in Chattanooga in 1932, Krystal restaurants—with their immediately recognizable Krystal hamburgers—have become more than sparkling-clean eateries where friendly employees serve up fresh, delicious food. Krystal has become a cultural icon, and an experience that virtually every man, woman, and child in the Southeast has shared. ✳ Nearly everyone in the region has a Krystal memory: taking a date out for a sack full of Krystals; a young boy discovering his first Krystal corn dog; a friend eating 15 Krystals in a single sitting to break a high school record. The Krystal brand—and the great food, service, value, and setting for which it stands—has taken a prominent place in the Southeast's cultural landscape.

Krystal Company Chairman and CEO Phil Sanford sums it up best when he says, "You don't go to McDonald's to buy a McDonald, or to Burger King to buy a Burger King. Only at Krystal do you actually buy a Krystal, which means that when our customers think of us, they think immediately of our product: fresh, hot, small, square. The two have become intertwined—that's how uniquely flavorful, memorable, and pleasurable the Krystal experience is."

Substance and Style

But Krystal is more than a cultural icon. In the six years between 1992 and 1997, the chain added 91 restaurants—an increase of 37 percent—in the 10 southeastern states that make up the firm's base of operations. Sanford believes the company has far to go before achieving market saturation: "The growth potential within these 10 states alone is virtually unlimited. During the next two years, we expect to build 25 new, company-owned restaurants—including three in Chattanooga—and to see an even stronger expansion of our franchise operations. We're particularly pleased to be able to add restaurants in Chattanooga, a city with which we feel a special kinship. In fact, we see Chattanooga's rebirth not as just an increased opportunity for us to grow, but as a parallel to the exciting innovations we're making throughout our organization and within our product lines."

Sanford believes that for any business to succeed, it must be different, better, and special. These three principles guide his stewardship of the Krystal brand name. "We will always stand for fresh, mouth-watering food; real value for the money; people-pleasing service; and Krystal-clean surroundings," he says. "Anything we do to enhance that winning formula has to be something that continues to make us different, better, and special. That's why we've been careful to apply those principles to all our latest initiatives, whether it's updating the inner and outer design of our restaurants; developing tasty, new products; creating innovative packaging; introducing new technologies; or training our people to be the best servers in the industry."

Krystal Company Chairman and CEO Phil Sanford believes that for any business to succeed, it must be different, better, and special. These three principles guide his stewardship of the Krystal brand name.

The Krystal brand—and the great food, service, and value for which it stands—has taken a prominent place in the Southeast's cultural landscape.

NEARLY EVERYONE IN THE SOUTHEAST HAS A KRYSTAL MEMORY: TAKING A DATE OUT FOR A SACK FULL OF KRYSTALS; A YOUNG BOY DISCOVERING HIS FIRST KRYSTAL CORN DOG; A FRIEND EATING 15 KRYSTALS IN A SINGLE SITTING TO BREAK A HIGH SCHOOL RECORD. AND WITH ITS EMPHASIS ON SATISFACTION, THE KRYSTAL COMPANY IS SURE TO ENJOY CONTINUED SUCCESS AND GROWTH FOR MANY YEARS TO COME.

A KRYSTAL CLEAR FUTURE

The Krystal Company is moving forward with initiatives in many areas. A brand-new restaurant design has been developed that pays homage to the traditional Krystal look, while showcasing the company's modern, new image. Future restaurants will sport this fresh, new face, inviting both longtime Krystal customers and hungry newcomers to stop in for a meal.

Krystal has also introduced a new item to its menu—the Krystal Chik, a lightly breaded chicken breast fillet served hot and fresh with mayonnaise and a savory pickle on a steamed Krystal bun. This mouthwatering combination lives up to its promotional slogan, Fresh, Hot, Small, Square.

Krystal has always been an innovator with its product packaging. Krystal boxes, for example, provide perfect little "houses" that make take-out orders easy and convenient. Now, the company has gone a step farther with the Krystal Go Cup, specially designed drink cups that fit perfectly in the drink wells of car consoles. Sanford says, "This built-in convenience is what being different, better, and special is all about."

Sanford is also convinced that technology will play an increasingly important role at The Krystal Company. "Technology will allow us to allocate our resources more effectively in the marketplace. Technology improvements will provide better decision making for our managers at all levels, while helping produce product and deliver services more efficiently. More technology in our restaurants will ultimately reduce our operating costs, which will then support even more growth of the Krystal system."

Sanford has an equally simple yet powerful formula regarding Krystal employees: "I want our employees to say that this is a great place to work, that they feel good working here, that they are rewarded according to their performance, and that all employees are treated fairly."

With its emphasis on satisfaction—for both the customer and its employees—The Krystal Company is sure to enjoy continued success and growth for many years to come.

M

cKEE FOODS CORPORATION WAS FOUNDED IN CHATTANOOGA IN 1934 when a young couple with a big dream pawned their new truck and bought Jack's Cookie Company with a down payment of $288 and a lot of hope. The couple were O.D. and Ruth McKee, and their small bakery is now McKee Foods Corporation, the manufacturer of America's number one snack cake, the Little Debbie brand. How this bakery grew from five employees and a few thousand dollars in yearly sales to more than 5,000 employees and more than $825 million in annual sales is an inspirational story of determination, focus, confidence, and faith.

O.D. McKee was born near Dixon, Mississippi, to Pinkney and Malissa Foy. Malissa died three weeks after O.D.'s birth and Pinkney, faced with the challenge of raising this new baby and five other children alone, allowed O.D. to be adopted by Malissa's cousin Finis McKee and his wife, Annie Laurie. The McKees gave him the name Oather Dorris, and he became the second child in a family that would eventually include six children.

O.D.'s budding entrepreneurial spirit kept him afloat financially during his college years at Southern Junior College, now Southern Adventist University. He gathered clothes for a dry cleaner, collected watches to be repaired by a jeweler, cut hair in his room, worked in the infirmary, and did janitorial work. But an entrepreneur needs a stable partner and O.D. found the perfect partner in his wife, Ruth, who was a beauty, charming and musical, the catch of the campus. Their marriage took place in 1928, and the pair soon found themselves—like nearly everyone else—struggling their way through the Great Depression.

O.D. began selling Virginia Dare five-cent cakes in Chattanooga in 1933. On Mondays, he would take out the backseat to use the car for his deliveries. On Fridays, the car seat went back in, and the 1928 Whippet again became the family car. That year O.D. learned some very valuable lessons—he could sell,

he loved being his own boss, and there seemed to be a market for baked goods, even during a depression.

A RISK TAKER

McKee Foods owes a great deal of its success to O.D.'s risk-taking spirit. At some point, he heard a quote attributed to Thomas Edison, "If there's a better way to do it, find it." O.D. applied this dictum to his business, always looking for better ways, whether they involved improving machinery design, inventing new products, or improving processes and procedures.

Another reason for the company's success is Ruth McKee. An entrepreneur needs a partner who will help him see what is reasonable, insist on return on investment, and deal with the sometimes boring and routine responsibilities that can't be avoided in the day-to-day running of a business. Ruth provided all of these things for O.D. She also headed the company's personnel department and later took on the purchasing responsibilities, proving to have

O.D. AND RUTH McKEE FOUNDED THE McKEE FOODS CORPORATION IN 1934 (TOP).

O.D. McKEE BEGAN HIS BUSINESS SELLING VIRGINIA DARE FIVE-CENT CAKES IN CHATTANOOGA IN 1933, USING THE BACKSEAT OF HIS 1928 WHIPPET TO MAKE DELIVERIES. FROM THIS HUMBLE BEGINNING CAME McKEE FOODS, A COMPANY WITH MORE THAN $825 MILLION IN ANNUAL SALES (BOTTOM).

Baxter is vice president, accounting. Jackson L. Case III is vice president, operating; Stephen W. Lawrence is vice president, engineering; Steve L. Clark is vice president, general services; and Richard L. Garner is vice president, pricing and policy development.

The Electric Power Board is the largest taxpayer in Chattanooga and Hamilton County. For fiscal year 1996-1997, payments in lieu of taxes to the towns and counties in its service area amounted to more than $6.5 million.

LOW-COST, RELIABLE POWER

One of the nation's largest debt-free municipal power distributors, EPB is committed to low-cost, reliable electric power. A 1997 rate increase of 2.97 percent followed 10 years of stable rates for EPB customers. The rate increase, DePriest says, was necessitated by three factors: depletion of EPB resources due to seven major storm restorations be-

ginning with the blizzard of 1993, the rising cost of doing business, and the necessity for funds to continue the organization's commitment to building and maintaining its power distribution system. As of June 30, 1998, EPB's depreciated plant value totaled more than $187 million.

According to DePriest, a stable rate structure is essential to continued economic development throughout the service area. EPB's commitment to stimulating growth is evidenced in its $2.5 million investment in the state-of-the-art Supervisory Control and Data Acquisition (SCADA) system that will facilitate rapid response in storm restoration efforts, as well as more efficient day-to-day operations. And, DePriest points out, EPB already has a cutting-edge mapping system in operation that is unequaled among power distributors in the Southeast.

These improvements to EPB's electric power distribution system will prove beneficial as the organiza-

tion moves into the high-tech world of telecommunications. With a 10-mile loop of fiber-optic cable already installed at its facilities in downtown Chattanooga, EPB has positioned itself to serve customers with high-speed data transmission needs and is prepared to enter the local telephone market as a provider before the millennium.

"Our state-of-the-art SCADA and mapping systems are expensive, and we have invested a great deal of effort to improve and upgrade the power distribution system," DePriest says. "Those expenses are essential to further growth and economic development in our community, as is our entry into the telecommunications arena. We are committed to providing telecommunications services with the same affordable costs and high levels of customer service that our electric customers rightfully expect from us."

Alexian Village of Tennessee

COVERING MORE THAN 33 ACRES ATOP SIGNAL MOUNTAIN, JUST 20 MINUTES from Chattanooga, Alexian Village of Tennessee fills the eye with a woodland view of a spacious and breathtaking campus. "Village" is an apt word to describe this community where residents play an important role in coordinating the activities and programs. The facility has everything from a post office to a 24-hour television station—not to mention a panoramic view of the surrounding Tennessee River Gorge. Altogether, these features provide the setting for a dynamic option in senior residences, including independent living, assisted living, and intermediate and long-term skilled care. The Village also provides exceptional, professional care for Alzheimer's residents off campus, known as Alexian Brothers Valley Residence.

In 1936, the Alexian Brothers Order, dedicated to the care and comfort of the elderly, converted the luxurious Signal Mountain Inn into a home for elderly men. The Brothers provided meals, laundry, and nursing services. In 1950, the Alexian Brothers Order moved its worldwide headquarters and Generalate to the Signal Mountain campus, where they remain today. In 1964, the Brothers made the decision to open their doors to the care of women, as well as men. And, in 1979, this growing collective envisioned the continuing need for quality senior lifestyle choices and created a life care facility as part of Alexian Brothers.

THE VILLAGE

One of the first of its kind, the Village is committed to quality, active senior living. Its atrium-designed Central Community Center offers not one, but four floors for resident use. An extensive ceramics room, complete with five kilns, is accessible 24 hours a day, and the completely equipped woodworking shop has produced many of the resident-made bookshelves and cabinets in the common areas of the Village. An auditorium, three chapels, three game rooms, a pool room, a craft room, a health club with a spa, a library, meeting spaces, an outdoor pool, and a beauty parlor are just a few of the other amenities. Resident-run activities include an investment club, a travel club, water aerobic classes, and a computer group. For many residents here, retirement means active relaxation.

Spanning out and around from the community center are immaculate, exactingly built apartments where independent living residents make their homes. Each luxurious apartment includes a balcony or a patio, and many residents are active gardeners. There's even a raised bed for growing vegetables that is very popular among the residents. The Brow View building provides sweeping views of the so-called Tennessee Grand Canyon sloping below. Residents in all the apartments enjoy one meal a day of their choosing in the expansive main dining room, which includes gracious table-side service, as part of the Alexian Village experience.

Perhaps the most comforting of all, when a resident moves into an apartment at Alexian Village, the health care comes with it. Other facilities include progressive fees associated with progressive care. At Alexian, should an independent living resident require more assistance, the appropriate level of care is included whether a resident needs assisted, intermediate, or long-term care. This frees a resident to appreciate the finer points of living in such a welcoming setting.

THE ALEXIAN VILLAGE OF TENNESSEE, LOCATED ATOP SIGNAL MOUNTAIN, HAS EVERYTHING FROM A POST OFFICE TO A 24-HOUR TELEVISION STATION—NOT TO MENTION A PANORAMIC VIEW OF THE SURROUNDING TENNESSEE RIVER GORGE.

THE WORLDWIDE HEADQUARTERS FOR THE ALEXIAN BROTHERS IS ALSO LOCATED ON SIGNAL MOUNTAIN.

MULTIPLE FACILITIES FOR CHANGING NEEDS

Alexian Inn, the Village's assisted living facility, is housed in the old Signal Mountain Inn, replete with crown moldings, 14-foot-tall ceilings, and three beautiful fireplaces. Although visually impressive, intimacy and privacy can be found in the cozy seating areas. The living services here are offered to those individuals who require occasional daily assistance with personal needs. The facility has its own private dining room where three meals a day are served table side. Residents furnish their own rooms for a homey, comfortable feel, and each room has a private bath.

The Alexian Health Care Center is staffed by RNs and LPNs 24 hours a day to offer intermediate and long-term skilled care. But emotional, environmental, and spiritual needs are equally addressed by the caring, professional staff. The center's color scheme is soft and feels cozy. There's a memory garden and gazebo with a reflecting pool where residents can spend some time outdoors, and the center has its own dining room. Respect and compassion for all is part of the philosophy that makes the health care center an excellent alternative to traditional homes.

For Alzheimer's residents, the Alexian Brothers Health System, working with the Southeast Tennessee Alzheimer's Association, has designed a unique, specialized residence consisting of three 14-bedroom homes and a 20-person adult day care center—all under one roof, known as Alexian Brothers Valley Residence. Alzheimer's residents are returned to a secure, homelike environment—maximizing independence with assistance while minimizing the causes of agitation.

ALEXIAN BROTHERS COMMUNITY SERVICES

Sponsoring the Program of All-Inclusive Care for the Elderly (PACE) has allowed the Alexian Brothers to expand their ministry to encompass the poor and the frail. Enrollees must be at least 55 years old and certified as eligible for nursing home care. Alexian's goal is to maximize each enrollee's autonomy and continued community residence, while providing all medical care and long-term care services in the most appropriate setting for the individual.

The Alexian community, inspired by the 700-year-old healing mission of the Alexian Brothers to the elderly, provides a continuum of services to residents that maximize dignity and independence. Rooted in the Catholic tradition of caring, the staff of the Alexian System is committed to promoting the well-being of its residents and of those it serves in the surrounding community through the delivery of high-quality services. Accordingly, the Alexian System was the first health care facility in Tennessee to be accredited through the Continuing Care Accreditation Commission, sponsored by the American Association of Homes and Services for the Aging.

PERSONAL ATTENTION IS GIVEN TO EVERY RESIDENT IN THE ALEXIAN BROTHERS VALLEY RESIDENCE.

ALEXIAN VILLAGERS CONTINUE TO LEAD ACTIVE LIVES WITH ANNUAL WHITE-WATER RAFTING TRIPS ON THE NANTAHALA RIVER IN NORTH CAROLINA.

T.U. Parks Construction Company

HATTANOOGA-AREA BUILDINGS CONSTRUCTED BY T.U. PARKS Construction Company are impressive, to say the least: the Krystal and Tallan office buildings, Warehouse Row, Heritage Landing residential development, Mountain City Club, CARTA Shuttle Park North and South, Baylor School, Girls Preparatory School, and Newly Weds Foods and Bradley Memorial Hospital in Cleveland, Tennessee.

Also, with a specialty in health care since 1970, Parks has had engagements with all of the area hospital organizations—the list could go on and on.

Why all the success? Because people know with Parks Construction as their contractor, the job will be done right. Such confidence accounts for the extremely high rate of repeat business that Parks Construction enjoys, and the impressive number of jobs the firm is directly awarded without need for competitive bidding.

At the core of this customer confidence is Parks Construction's philosophy. "We expect to be part of the team—working closely with the owner and the architect until that final project is realized and everybody is happy with it," says Larry Parks, president and grandson of founder T.U. Parks. "We want to grow and do more and bigger jobs, but never at the expense of our personal relationship with our customers. An officer of the company is involved in every project."

Quality Craftsmanship

The unmistakable mark of quality craftsmanship has been the defining element of Parks Construction since the firm's inception in 1944. T.U. Parks, who died in 1973, was a carpenter who was respected from the outset by associates and friends for his craftsmanship and dedication to quality work at a good price. His skill and commitment were handed down to his sons, C.A. and Homer, who from the mid-1950s oversaw the company's growth and expansion. Homer Parks died in 1987, while C.A. Parks continues to actively serve the company as chairman of the board.

Throughout the years, Parks Construction has pursued a course of planned growth—a cautious approach that is echoed in the careful, methodical way the company handles each project. As a result, it has progressed from a one-man operation to a corporation known throughout the South for its personal attention to detail and diverse construction experience.

Parks Construction has earned a reputation for staying in close contact with clients from the moment a project begins through its completion. The firm's management staff has amassed more than two centuries of combined construction expertise, while its field superintendents offer more than 350 years of combined tenure. These qualities enable Parks Construction to complete building projects—from remodeling and additions to multimillion-dollar undertakings—within budget and on time.

Pervading all of the company's accomplishments, though, are the never forgotten words of T.U. Parks as he described his approach to business so many years ago. "Be aggressive, but be fair," he said. "And whatever you do, never stop learning the business." With its ever growing list of satisfied customers, T.U. Parks Construction Company intends to continue learning for a long time to come.

SISKIN STEEL AND SUPPLY COMPANY HAS BEEN A T.U. PARKS CONSTRUCTION COMPANY CLIENT FOR MORE THAN 35 YEARS (TOP).

THE UNMISTAKABLE MARK OF QUALITY CRAFTSMANSHIP HAS BEEN THE DEFINING ELEMENT OF PARKS CONSTRUCTION SINCE THE FIRM'S INCEPTION IN 1944. THE CHAPEL OF THE BAYLOR SCHOOL IN CHATTANOOGA AND THE ATRIUM OF BRADLEY MEMORIAL HOSPITAL IN CLEVELAND, TENNESSEE, ARE JUST TWO EXAMPLES OF THE SKILL AND COMMITMENT OF PARKS CONSTRUCTION (BOTTOM LEFT AND RIGHT).

THE CENTER FOR SPORTS MEDICINE & ORTHOPAEDICS WAS FOUNDED IN 1947 as the Chattanooga Orthopaedic Group. As the practice grew, its primary focus gradually turned to sports medicine. In 1987, this facilitated the construction of a new building specifically designed to address athletes' needs. This modern concept brought physical therapists, athletic trainers, and orthopaedic physicians together under one roof. The new center was quickly recognized in the community for paving the way for safer athletics, as well as for preparing athletes for peak performance after an injury.

Even before the new facility was built, the center began an outreach program for area schools, putting certified athletic trainers on-site at the practices and games of area high school football teams. The outreach program has since expanded, covering all sports for more than a dozen high schools, universities, and professional sports teams, including the AA Southern League Chattanooga Lookouts baseball team. The center has maintained this long-term commitment to the Chattanooga community for more than 10 years with no costs incurred by the teams or coaches of area schools.

A TEAM OF SPECIALISTS

In 1994, the doctors recognized the need for specialty orthopaedics in the tristate region and began recruiting physicians with board certification and fellowship training in orthopaedics focused on a particular part of the body. Since that time, they have added two spine specialists, a specialist in total joint reconstruction, a hand specialist, and a specialist in conditions of the foot and ankle, as well as a primary care sports medicine specialist. The additional training and the heightened level of expertise have resulted in a reputation that attracts patients of all ages, regardless of athletic ability.

Among the center's other distinguishing features is its self-funded Foundation for Research. The foundation is a separate corporation dedicated to clinical orthopaedic research and education. Opportunities for medical and premedical students are plentiful and allow students to participate in provocative research as they pursue their educational goals. The students and doctors then submit articles for publication in national and international medical journals. Often, these publications lead to invitations for presentations by the center's physicians at medical education conferences. Orthopaedic medical information is also accessible to physicians and patients on the center's Web site at www.chattortho.com.

The center supports academics through a teaching role with East Tennessee State University James H. Quillen College of Medicine Family Practice Residency. The residents study with the physicians to learn more about orthopaedic conditions and the special knowledge required to treat particular limbs or areas of the body. The magnitude of the center's academic efforts has been rewarded by requests from authors to write the orthopaedic chapters in clinical textbooks utilized in medical schools.

Combining research, education, and community outreach, the Center for Sports Medicine & Orthopaedics will continue to be a valuable resource for the city of Chattanooga and the surrounding tristate area, as it has been for the last half century.

(TOP ROW, LEFT TO RIGHT) ALAN C. ODOM, M.D.; KURT M. CHAMBLESS, M.D.; N. EARL MCELHENEY, M.D.; (MIDDLE ROW, LEFT TO RIGHT) SCOTT D. HODGES, D.O.; W. TIMOTHY BALLARD, M.D.; ROBERT D. MASTEY, M.D.; (BOTTOM ROW, LEFT TO RIGHT) S. CRAIG HUMPHREYS, M.D.; JOHN H. CHROSTOWSKI, M.D.; TRACY R. RAY, M.D.

THE CENTER'S PHYSICIANS ARE DEDICATED TO THE ONGOING PURSUIT OF CLINICAL STUDIES THROUGH THE FOUNDATION FOR RESEARCH (BOTTOM).

DuPont Nylon
Chattanooga Plant

SOME 60 YEARS AGO, THE MERCHANDISING EXPERTS WHO FROWNED ON the latest DuPont fibers invention had no idea the product was about to trigger near riots in stores across the country. American women, who clamored to buy 64 million pairs of nylons the first year, weren't the only ones impressed with the lightweight material; the government was soon ordering the synthetic fiber for parachutes, tire cord, and tugboat ropes.

Demand was so great that in 1948, DuPont, headquartered in Wilmington since its establishment in 1802, opened its third nylon yarn plant in Chattanooga, with 900 employees and an annual production rate of 8 million pounds. For more than 50 years, the Chattanooga DuPont plant has remained one of the city's top economic catalysts and most respected corporate neighbors.

The facility, which today employs approximately 1,600 people and produces about 250 million pounds each year, has expanded several times and now manufactures three main types of nylon: transportation yarns for tires, conveyor belts, webbing, and ropes; Cordura® yarns for sports fabrics, luggage, and duffel bags; and apparel yarns for clothing, flags, parachutes, and, of course, hosiery. Engineering polymers are also developed at the Chattanooga facility for use in plastic moldings, auto parts, and food processing.

PROTECTING THE EARTH

Going beyond simply increasing its profit margin, DuPont is deeply committed to an ambitious goal of zero injuries, zero waste, with environmental standards that go far beyond legal requirements. Whenever possible, materials are reused and recycled to conserve resources and minimize the need for treatment or disposal. Top priority is given to reducing or eliminating industrial emissions.

In step with a companywide ecological program launched by DuPont Chairman Ed Woolard in 1989, the plant maintains a 200-acre wildlife sanctuary for great blue herons, hawks, owls, foxes, songbirds, hummingbirds, and other native animals. The refuge was the first site in Tennessee to be certified by the National Institute for Urban Wildlife and the only one in the state to receive Highest Habitat certification from the Wildlife Habitat Enhancement Council in 1991.

The Green Team, a group of employees who regularly work on environmental issues affecting the plant and the community, is credited for many of these achievements. The team implements a variety of projects, from recycling programs to Earth Day celebrations to the cultivation of a butterfly garden at the front entrance. The company's open-door policy encourages all employees to offer ideas for improving operations throughout the plant.

Also a widely recognized leader in manufacturing safety, the Chattanooga facility has received numerous local, state, and national awards, including World Safety Records in 1959, 1967, and 1980.

GIVING BACK TO THE COMMUNITY

At DuPont, community support is still as strong as the durable nylon filament that caused such a sensation in 1938. Ongoing sponsorships include a Safe Kids program in area schools; the DuPont Community Initiatives Funds (DCIF) to support educational and environmental projects in Hamilton County; and major contributions to the Tennessee Aquarium, Creative Discovery Museum, Tennessee River Gorge Trust, and other institutions.

In 1997, the Chattanooga DuPont site again drew accolades when it announced the largest new capital investment in the state—$250 million in upgrades and the creation of 300 new jobs. In the words of the 1946 *Chattanooga Times* editorial heralding the birth of the plant, this news is "rich in implications for the future growth of our community." It is just another step DuPont has taken to improve the quality of life in Chattanooga.

DUPONT NYLON IS DEEPLY COMMITTED TO AN AMBITIOUS GOAL OF ZERO INJURIES, ZERO WASTE, WITH ENVIRONMENTAL STANDARDS THAT GO FAR BEYOND LEGAL REQUIREMENTS.

1949-1998

1951	Hunter Museum of American Art
1952	Memorial Hospital/Chattanooga Heart Institute
1956	Insurance Planning & Service Company, Inc.
1960	Arthur Andersen
1960	Ernst & Young LLP
1964	Covenant College
1966	Petty & Landis, P.C.
1969	Allied Arts of Greater Chattanooga
1971	Columbia/HCA Chattanooga Region
1971	Joseph Decosimo and Company, LLP
1975	AAA Courier Service
1983	Mountain City Realtors
1983	Volunteer Bank & Trust Company
1983	WUSY-FM/US-101
1985	U.S. Xpress Enterprises, Inc.
1986	Chattanooga Neighborhood Enterprise, Inc.
1987	Ballet Tennessee/Baker-Van Cura Ballet Centre
1989	Chattanooga Choo-Choo Holiday Inn
1990	Metropolitan Security, Inc.
1991	Bluff View Art District
1992	Daniel+Douglas+Norcross
1992	Tennessee Aquarium
1993	AmSouth Bancorporation
1995	Adams Hilborne Mansion Inn & Restaurant
1995	Docu-Shred
1996	e.spire

THE HUNTER MUSEUM OF AMERICAN ART HOUSES THE FINEST COLLECTION of American paintings and sculpture in the Southeast. Opened in 1951 and built on a 90-foot limestone bluff overlooking the Tennessee River, the complex features two distinct buildings—a turn-of-the-century mansion and a dramatic contemporary structure. ✳ The 1906 classical revival mansion, once the home of George Thomas Hunter,

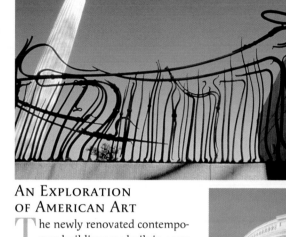

philanthropist and owner of the world's first Coca-Cola bottling company, is the heart of the Hunter Museum. The mansion houses earlier works by such well-known artists as Albert Bierstadt, George Inness, and Thomas Sully, to name just a few. The classical revival architectural style of the mansion includes the original fireplaces, hardwood floors, wall moldings, hand-carved woodwork, foyer chandelier, sconces, and fixtures over the grand staircase. Many of the ornamental details utilize egg-and-dart, acanthus-leaf, and fruit-and-flower motifs popularized by architects of that period.

Early 18th- and 19th-century artwork is exhibited in the mansion, including American impressionists Mary Cassatt, Childe Hassam, and, from the Hudson River School—perhaps the best-known style of the period—Asher B. Durand and Thomas Cole. The mansion also showcases an outstanding collection of notable American photographers, including Ansel Adams.

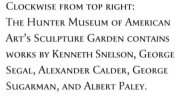

CLOCKWISE FROM TOP RIGHT:
THE HUNTER MUSEUM OF AMERICAN ART'S SCULPTURE GARDEN CONTAINS WORKS BY KENNETH SNELSON, GEORGE SEGAL, ALEXANDER CALDER, GEORGE SUGARMAN, AND ALBERT PALEY.

THE 1906 CLASSICAL REVIVAL PORTICO OF THE HUNTER MUSEUM WELCOMES VISITORS.

ONE OF THE HUNTER MUSEUM'S NEW TRADITIONAL GALLERIES HOUSES WORKS SUCH AS MARY CASSATT'S *Baby Bill in Cap and Shift, Held by His Nurse.*

AN EXPLORATION OF AMERICAN ART

The newly renovated contemporary building was built in 1975 and houses a unique and diverse collection tracing the development of American art from the early 20th century to the contemporary period. The building was constructed of cast-in-place architectural concrete with a sand-blasted exterior in the brutalist style of Marcel Breur, and contrasts with the mansion while blending with its location on—and literally in—the rocky bluff.

The contemporary galleries host changing traveling exhibitions and a wide variety of educational and public programs such as gallery lectures, art classes, concerts, films, and children's programs. They also house artwork ranging from Ashcan School artists George Luks and Robert Henri to late-20th-century paintings by Andy Warhol, Jack Beal, Hans Hofmann, Helen Frankenthaler, and many others.

The Hunter Museum has a very distinguished collection of contemporary studio glass. Pieces by Dale Chihuly, Harvey Littleton, and William Morris can be found in this gallery. A major monumental site-specific piece by Howard Ben Tré was dedicated in 1998 and is the centerpiece of the distinguished collection.

A must-see is the Hunter's Sculpture Garden. This outdoor gallery contains sculptures by Kenneth

Snelson, George Segal, Alexander Calder, George Sugarman, and Albert Paley.

The Hunter Museum also sponsors—with help from loyal volunteers—many special events and educational programs annually. They include Spectrum, an annual art auction; Christmas At The Hunter; First Friday; Family Day; ARTstravaganza; Art After Work; Casino Night; Art Camp; and ArtScene, the museum's high school art program. Symphony music and other performance programs are also featured.

With the beautifully restored 1906 classic revival building and the newly renovated contemporary building, the Hunter Museum enters the 21st century with a great tradition and an optimistic and exciting future.

THE NAME ARTHUR ANDERSEN HAS BECOME SYNONYMOUS WITH professionalism, outstanding technical knowledge, and dedication to client service. From its first location in the Maclellan Building in 1960, to its current home in the Republic Centre, the Chattanooga office has served as accountant, tax consultant, and business adviser to many of the area's most prominent companies,

executives, and other leading Chattanooga residents. Arthur Andersen's commitment to the growth and success of privately owned family businesses, midsize public corporations, innovative start-ups, and their stakeholders is legendary.

While Arthur Andersen is an international firm, the Chattanooga office is a local office committed to the growth and advancement of Chattanooga. Whether it is through participation in United Way's Day of Caring, adopting needy families at Christmas, or support of the arts and local charities, area Arthur Andersen personnel contribute to making Chattanooga a better place to live.

When Arthur Andersen founded the firm in 1913, he said, "We want to measure our contribution more by the quality of the service rendered than by whether we are making a good living out of it." Today, quality is still the firm's number one focus, as it strives continuously to understand, meet, and exceed clients' needs and expectations.

"Arthur Andersen works to acquire and share knowledge—demonstrating how to improve performance in management, business processes, operations, information technology, finance, and change management," says Jeff Green, managing partner of the Chattanooga office. "This helps our clients grow and profit."

The "One Firm" Firm

Arthur Andersen has 363 offices in 78 countries. However, this global presence involves more than simply occupying space; it is also an attitude. With a unique organizational structure, common methods, and shared values, Arthur Andersen is able to serve its clients, wherever they are located, as one firm. The Chattanooga team works with more than 60,000 Arthur Andersen team members—across boundaries of competencies, function, and geog-

raphies—to provide each client a complete, multidisciplinary solution.

Beyond the conventional professional services firm, Arthur Andersen provides numerous services within the following categories: Assurance and Business Advisory services; Business Consulting; Economic and Financial Consulting; and Tax and Business Advisory services. The firm works to assure the integrity and reliability of a client's information, assess the effectiveness of underlying processes, and help identify, measure, and control a wide range of risks.

Arthur Andersen's business solutions help its worldwide client base achieve measurable performance improvement and lasting change. By applying business and industry knowledge, the firm conceives and executes financial strategies that are aligned with corporate objectives and enable them to improve performance, shape competitive advantage, and create shareholder value. The firm also utilizes its resources and skills to help clients address the complex issues of taxation, mergers

and acquisitions, and debt and equity offerings.

The Future of the Firm

Looking to the future, Arthur Andersen has created KnowledgeSpace℠, a service that combines the firm's proprietary knowledge with relevant Internet information on a Web site available to subscribers. This service transforms the Internet's vast volume of information into a practical business tool by delivering timely and relevant information. At the same time, subscribers are connected to the firm's professionals, knowledge assets, and solutions.

"Arthur Andersen continually helps companies improve business performance by making it easier to share and apply knowledge resources," says Green. "From showing clients how to perform business tasks faster to helping them manage their own knowledge assets, this initiative distinguishes Arthur Andersen as the first place to go for business knowledge."

THE CENTER FOR PROFESSIONAL EDUCATION, A 151-ACRE CAMPUS FACILITY LOCATED IN ST. CHARLES, ILLINOIS, DEMONSTRATES ARTHUR ANDERSEN'S COMMITMENT TO THE CONTINUOUS EDUCATION AND TRAINING OF ITS PERSONNEL (LEFT).

THE CHATTANOOGA TEAM WORKS WITH MORE THAN 60,000 ARTHUR ANDERSEN TEAM MEMBERS—ACROSS BOUNDARIES OF COMPETENCIES, FUNCTION, AND GEOGRAPHIES—TO PROVIDE EACH CLIENT A COMPLETE, MULTIDISCIPLINARY SOLUTION. LOCAL CLIENTS SUCH AS MILLER INDUSTRIES, INC. BENEFIT FROM THIS GLOBAL PRESENCE (RIGHT).

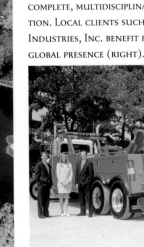

ANCHORED BY FAITH AND HERITAGE AND FOCUSED ON THE FUTURE, Memorial Hospital has achieved regional recognition as one of the most advanced medical facilities in the Southeast. The not-for-profit hospital opened in 1952 and has steadily strengthened its ministry of healing by responding with insight, excellence, and compassion to changing health care needs. The hospital has been guided by the values of the Sisters of Charity of Nazareth, Kentucky, who developed a multimillion-dollar health system spanning three states. In 1997, the Sisters of Charity of Nazareth partnered with Catholic Health Initiatives, the largest not-for-profit health system in the United States.

Today, as one of a network of 70 hospitals in 22 states, Memorial continues to be dedicated to Christian values and to offer advanced technology and treatment options, along with a complete range of services for health and wellness, including preventive and early detection programs.

HIGH STANDARD OF EXCELLENCE

Memorial is the preeminent provider of cardiac care in the region. Affiliated with the Chattanooga Heart Institute, a multimillion-dollar cardiovascular facility on the hospital campus, Memorial's commitment to excellence in this specialty is all-encompassing. Cardiac care services include prevention, emergency services, state-of-the-art technology for diagnosis and treatment, the most extensive cardiac surgery program in the area, and outstanding cardiopulmonary rehabilitation services.

A regional leader in cancer care, Memorial is on the cutting edge in technology and treatment, while providing strong spiritual and emotional support for families and patients. The H. Clay Evans Johnson Cancer Center on the hospital campus offers convenient access to all cancer services, including some of the most promising diagnostic and treatment options currently available in cancer research.

Memorial's 75,000-square-foot surgery center provides innovative, responsive, and continually advancing resources for all specialties. Memorial also has surgical programs at Memorial Atrium Surgical Center, a freestanding joint-venture facility near Hamilton Place; at Memorial North Park; and at Women's East Pavilion, which is operated by Memorial and Erlanger. Obstetric needs are specifically addressed at Women's Pavilion.

Other areas of expertise at Memorial include orthopedic and neurological services, pediatrics, general medicine, diabetes, and emergency services. Memorial's professional ambulances are stationed in key locations for prompt response to emergency needs. The Emergency Center features 23 private treatment rooms, including a five-room cardiac suite, trauma rooms, and special treatment rooms for children.

BUILDING A HEALTHIER COMMUNITY

To ensure that all areas of the community have access to health care and to promote wellness of body, mind, and spirit, Memorial works with other organizations to develop innovative and beneficial programs and facilities.

Memorial and the YMCA partnered to build the Hamilton Family YMCA and Memorial Center for Health. The hospital provides convenient primary care services, like Memorial North Shore Health Center, in areas of the county that were previously underserved. Educational and support programs for clergy are offered at the hospital, along with parish nursing and Stephen Ministry training, to help churches strengthen their health ministries. The hospital works with agencies like Catholic Charities and the Samaritan Center to provide clinical and support services to different sections of the community. Screenings and health education programs are available to all on a continuing basis.

"We are deeply committed to Christ's example of healing," says Memorial CEO Clark Taylor. "Fidelity to the gospel urges us to respect human dignity and promote wellness of body, mind, and spirit. There is a difference at Memorial."

CLOCKWISE FROM TOP RIGHT: THE MAIN CAMPUS OF MEMORIAL HOSPITAL IS LOCATED IN THE GLENWOOD NEIGHBORHOOD AT THE FOOT OF MISSIONARY RIDGE.

DR. MALCOLM DANIELL PERFORMS A CORONARY BYPASS AT MEMORIAL. DR. DANIELL CAME FROM BAYLOR UNIVERSITY TO ASSIST WITH THE HOSPITAL'S FIRST OPEN-HEART SURGERY IN 1972 AND HAS HELPED DEVELOP MEMORIAL'S OUTSTANDING CARDIAC PROGRAM.

"WE ARE DEEPLY COMMITTED TO CHRIST'S EXAMPLE OF HEALING," SAYS MEMORIAL CEO CLARK TAYLOR. "FIDELITY TO THE GOSPEL URGES US TO RESPECT HUMAN DIGNITY AND PROMOTE WELLNESS OF BODY, MIND, AND SPIRIT. THERE IS A DIFFERENCE AT MEMORIAL."

CHARLES TURNER

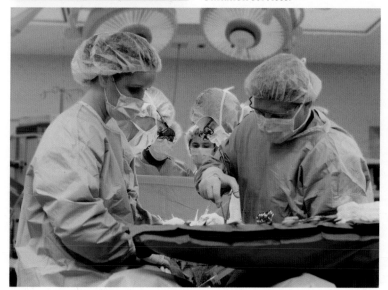

T

HE RESULT OF A VISION THAT BEGAN 15 YEARS AGO, CHATTANOOGA Heart Institute was established with a single purpose. Founded in 1992, the Heart Institute's mission is to reduce the incidence and mortality rate of heart and vascular diseases by developing and promoting advancements in prevention, diagnosis, and treatment. The institute also strives to reduce recovery time for

those suffering from cardiovascular diseases.

But unlike many health care facilities, Chattanooga Heart Institute was also founded on a unique patient-centered philosophy. Because of this emphasis on patient well-being—combined with cutting-edge technology, top physicians, a cardiac and pulmonary rehabilitation facility, and ongoing research activities—the institute is regarded as a model for heart institutes of the future.

TOP-NOTCH SPECIALISTS AND TECHNOLOGY

The Heart Institute has attracted top heart and vascular specialists from all over the country. Board-certified with subspecialties, most of them have spent a significant amount of time in academic environments. This academic focus has helped the institute to provide many advancements in the diagnosis and treatment of cardiovascular disease for the Chattanooga region. In fact, institute physicians were the first in the area to explore the use of angioplasty, atherectomy, excimer laser treatments, intracoronary stent, cardiac electrophysiologic testing, radiofrequency ablation for arrhythmias, and the insertion of implanted cardioverter defibrillators (ICD).

The institute offers the most comprehensive invasive and noninvasive

tests and treatments in the Chattanooga area. The cardiovascular diagnostic department is equipped with the latest in nuclear imaging, echocardiography, and peripheral vascular imaging. As such, the institute can do a complete cardiovascular evaluation in one visit and under one roof.

Additionally, the Heart Institute provides comprehensive arrhythmia management. Complete in-house pacemaker care is also available, including monitoring and extensive in-office reprogramming. Transtelephonic pacemaker analysis even allows the institute to evaluate a patient's pacemaker over regular phone lines.

The institute also has a state-of-the-art outpatient digital catheterization laboratory. Cath lab patients can have procedures performed in the morning, be monitored in one of the facility's outpatient rooms during the afternoon, and be discharged the same day. This system reduces patient cost without compromising the patient's safety.

To ensure continued recovery, the institute's cardiac rehabilitation facility is outfitted with weight training equipment, treadmills, Stairmasters, exercise classes, and a staff that monitors the patient's progress. For preventive care, nutritional counseling and cholesterol management are also available on-site.

A RESEARCH CENTER

Research is an integral part of daily life at the institute. In fact, all institute physicians are involved in ongoing investigations, which allow area residents access to new treatments. Research generally involves Phase III, FDA-sanctioned experimental drug or device trials. Often, these trials entail such diverse agents as clot-dissolving drugs to treat heart attack victims and medications to control blood pressure, regulate heart rhythm, and lower cholesterol. The institute also evaluates the newest technological advances in pacemakers, implantable defibrillators, vascular stents, and similar devices.

All these efforts help the institute remain at the forefront of cardiovascular care and offer patients diagnostic and therapeutic choices that otherwise would only be available at major university centers. Through this comprehensive approach to cardiovascular care and research, the Chattanooga Heart Institute is helping to reduce the threat of heart and vascular diseases, and helping people attain a healthier and happier quality of life.

CLOCKWISE FROM TOP: KINSMAN E. WRIGHT, M.D., OVERSEES CHATTANOOGA HEART INSTITUTE'S STATE-OF-THE-ART OUTPATIENT DIGITAL CATHETERIZATION LABORATORY.

FOUNDED IN 1992, THE HEART INSTITUTE'S MISSION IS TO REDUCE THE INCIDENCE AND MORTALITY RATE OF HEART AND VASCULAR DISEASES BY DEVELOPING AND PROMOTING ADVANCEMENTS IN PREVENTION, DIAGNOSIS, AND TREATMENT.

TO ENSURE CONTINUED RECOVERY, THE INSTITUTE'S CARDIAC REHABILITATION FACILITY IS OUTFITTED WITH WEIGHT TRAINING EQUIPMENT, TREADMILLS, STAIRMASTERS, EXERCISE CLASSES, AND A STAFF THAT MONITORS THE PATIENT'S PROGRESS.

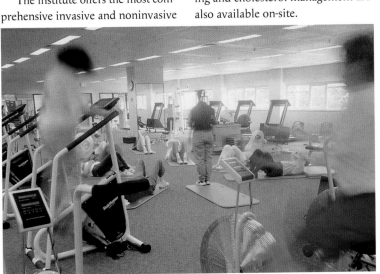

Insurance Planning & Service Company, Inc.

THOUGH MOST PEOPLE KNOW INSURANCE PLANNING & SERVICE COMPANY, Inc. simply as IPSCO, few people know the complexity and numerous services offered by the agency. Many may think that IPSCO simply puts together innovative insurance and benefits packages for employers; but in reality, the company is much more comprehensive in its scope, serving both the business and private sectors. "We're in the business of solving problems and providing solutions," says George "Con" Knox Jr., president of IPSCO.

IPSCO is also a strong provider of group and individual benefit packages to associations. A newer part of its business works to enhance membership to these associations by providing a wide range of noninsurance products, which it crafts to each association's needs as a method of adding value. Of course, this also means attracting new members and retaining satisfied members.

A History of Growth

Founder J. Walter Bishop Jr. created IPSCO as Independent Planning Service, Inc. The company was the first independent employee benefit firm in Tennessee. Some of the original clients of the firm include the Tennessee Bar Association and Tennessee Dental Association—still association clients of the firm today. Later, the firm also added other prominent professional associations as clients, including the Tennessee Medical Association in 1985 and the firm's first national association, Professional Convention Management Association, in 1992.

In 1956, Hugh C. Montgomery, a longtime employee of Provident Companies, Inc., joined Bishop to form IPSCO, with the "I" now standing for "insurance" instead of "independent." Together, they expanded the business of providing employer benefits packages and created a communications system that employers could use to help their employees understand the cost of employee benefit programs and the benefits themselves. In 1971, Knox joined the agency, and he recognized that the key to growing the firm was in expanding the association division. In 1980, Knox became president and owner of IPSCO.

Today, IPSCO tailors a wide range of choices and coverages for its clients, including group and individual medical insurance, liability coverage, life insurance, accidental death and dismemberment, workers' compensation, and disability. As a licensed third party administrator in Tennessee, IPSCO diligently services the products offered to its clients and delivers what the company calls "old-fashioned reliability with state-of-the-art service." The staff at IPSCO is hand-picked and long-term, and knows the business. In fact, IPSCO has two full-time programmers on staff who have created a program with an extensive database called WISDOM, just to ensure clients receive the best and most up-to-date service possible.

A Tailored Approach

IPSCO works with businesses to tailor benefit plans to each client—not just for today, but as the company's needs change. IPSCO is there to meet and anticipate each company's future needs and expectations. It does all the research, determines the risks, and puts together the most competitive quotes so the client can make an informed and secure choice. Since IPSCO is an independent agency, clients choose from the finest carriers with an emphasis on financial soundness.

Just as businesses need group plans, associations can benefit from group pricing for a wide array of products. With the endorsement of the Tennessee Society of Association Executives, IPSCO offers the same

CLOCKWISE FROM TOP:
IPSCO'S MANAGEMENT TEAM INCLUDES, (FROM LEFT) T. GORDON LOWE, CLU; V. CAROLYN NUCKOLS; GEORGE "CON" KNOX JR., CLU; RON B. MCCLISTER, CLU, CHFC; AND JEFFREY R. SMITH, CPA, CFP.

IPSCO IS A LICENSED THIRD-PARTY ADMINISTRATOR PERFORMING MANY OF THE FUNCTIONS OF AN INSURANCE CARRIER TO PROVIDE PROMPT SERVICE TO CLIENTELE.

IPSCO'S MARKETING DEPARTMENT UTILIZES THE IN-HOUSE, CUSTOM-DESIGNED DATABASE WISDOM, A SYSTEM FOR TRACKING AND MAINTAINING CLIENT INFORMATION.

insurance planning expertise to associations and more. Administering programs and updating databases can be a hefty task for some associations. IPSCO has up-to-the-minute programming and administering capabilities that ease the information burden so the association can concentrate on its business.

What's more, IPSCO's noninsurance products make membership in an association even more valuable. From discounted educational seminars to office supplies, car leasing to tax audit services, contracting long-distance services to Internet consulting, IPSCO can tailor a plan that offers the association member appropriate services at group prices. Gilbert R. Campbell, executive director of the Tennessee Bar Association, says, "We have been totally pleased with the diligent manner in which [IPSCO] administers our program and I heartily recommend them to any association." Noninsurance products are growing into an exciting and innovative part of IPSCO's

business. The company even manages its own in-house publishing and develops marketing pieces for each program. The firm's marketing director estimates that IPSCO sends out 16,000 to 20,000 personalized pieces per month.

Even though IPSCO administers plans to larger companies like Olan Mills and the Hamilton Medical Center, it understands the needs of small- to medium-size businesses as well. "We're a small business ourselves," says Knox. "We can appreciate their problems and special needs because we experience them, too." Creative and innovative solutions to plan problems is IPSCO's specialty, which positions the company to solve problems that other agencies sometimes can't. IPSCO owes

its success to building creative strategies and developing unique products that fit a particular business' needs. Through its membership and participation in the Professional Liability Underwriting Society, American College of Life Underwriters, and American Institute of Professional Association Group Insurance Administrators, the agency stays abreast of industry changes affecting its current and future clientele.

With additional offices in Memphis, Nashville, and Towson, Maryland, IPSCO is poised for growth well into the next century. As a reliable agency that is there to respond to each client's changing needs, IPSCO strikes the right balance between hometown friendliness and top-notch plan service.

CLOCKWISE FROM TOP:
IPSCO'S EXPERIENCED STAFF GATHERS IN FRONT OF THE 18,000-SQUARE-FOOT CHATTANOOGA HOME OFFICE.

ONGOING TRAINING IS AN INTEGRAL PART OF IPSCO'S MISSION STATEMENT.

LARGE CLIENTS, SUCH AS OLAN MILLS, LOOK TO IPSCO FOR FULL BENEFIT CONSULTING SERVICES.

ERNST & YOUNG LLP HAS BEEN A LEADING CONTRIBUTOR TO CHATTA-nooga's business and civic community since the local office of the firm was established on November 1, 1960. Like its national practice, Ernst & Young's Chattanooga office provides audit, tax, and consulting services for hundreds of clients, ranging from some of the area's largest firms to individual entrepreneurs just starting their businesses.

Ernst & Young is a leader among professional services organizations in delivering the ideas, solutions, and results that clients care about. The firm has the industry experience and technical skills to provide ideas and solutions that are tailored to clients' needs and deliver measurable

ERNST & YOUNG DELIVERS SERVICES USING A TEAM APPROACH THAT INTE-GRATES INDUSTRY KNOWLEDGE WITH SPECIALISTS IN VARIOUS DISCIPLINES.

results. With its size and global reach, Ernst & Young has the breadth and depth of resources to serve any company, wherever it does business.

Ernst & Young LLP is a result of the 1989 merger of two giants in the professional services industry, Ernst & Whinney and Arthur Young. The firm's worldwide presence includes more than 78,000 employees in more than 125 countries. In the United States, Ernst & Young has 29,000 professionals in 87 cities, making it the nation's largest integrated professional services firm, with more total revenues from accounting, audit, and tax services than any other U.S. firm.

A TEAM APPROACH

Because so many business issues are industry oriented, Ernst & Young delivers services using a team approach that integrates industry knowledge with specialists in various disciplines. In a similar fashion, the Entrepreneurial Services professionals focus on understanding and meeting the needs of owner-managed

companies. This industry specialization allows Ernst & Young to serve clients' needs more efficiently and comprehensively by concentrating talent and focusing the experience, knowledge, and skills of its professionals on the industries they know best.

Ernst & Young delivers a number of key services, including assurance and advisory services; strategic transaction assessment; tax services; and consulting services within the client's industry, including management consulting, health care consulting, financial advisory services, and regulatory and related services.

Ernst & Young operates on a fundamental principle that long has been a firm hallmark. According to Don Bailey, partner in the Chattanooga office, "The success of Ernst & Young and its clients are linked. We understand that we must bring value to our clients for our mutual success to continue. We are committed to continuous improvement in all that we do. We seek to attract, develop, and retain high-performance people, and to deliver the highest-quality work and value-added services responsive to our clients' needs and expectations."

Ernst & Young is also dedicated to the success of the Chattanooga community. The firm and its employees have established a long-standing leadership position in numerous civic and charitable organizations. Whether simply lending a hand or helping to plan, implement, and track the results of community projects, Ernst & Young works to positively affect the lives of the residents and business owners of Chattanooga.

By exceeding client expectations and being an exemplary corporate citizen, Ernst & Young looks forward to continuing its position as a leading local and worldwide integrated professional services firm.

FOR NEARLY FOUR DECADES, PETTY & LANDIS, P.C. HAS BEEN A PROUD member of the business community in the beautiful River City, a city of mountain vistas, valleys, and rivers punctuated by the bridges that connect the communities that make up this great region. These bridges, just as they connect and allow relationships between the city's communities, illustrate the very essence of Joe Petty's and W.E. "Buddy" Landis' deeply held commitment to building strong relationships with their clients. After all, strong relationships promote experienced, responsible, and innovative solutions.

Formed in November 1966, Petty & Landis wanted to offer its customers more than just the standard accounting services. Its primary objective, to help clients prosper and grow, has its roots in providing sound business advice. Along with traditional services—accounting, financial audits, unaudited services, and tax preparation—the two men realized that they could offer clients more comprehensive services that considered the clients' businesses and offered a well-rounded perspective.

Petty's and Landis' foresight proved extremely beneficial to their customers. In turn, as clients' businesses grew, so did their need for more complex accounting and consultative services. As a result, Petty & Landis expanded in size and in range of services, adding the expertise to handle its clients' increasingly sophisticated accounting and business management needs.

FULL SERVICE

During the late 1970s and 1980s, the changing business environment was focusing on mergers and acquisitions. Specifically in the soft drink bottling industry, Petty & Landis was able to provide its clients with the necessary guidance through complex transactions involving the engineering of leveraged buyouts, resolving complicated tax questions, and addressing other intricate accounting issues. It was during this period that these types of activities served as the ultimate catalyst that would create opportunities for the firm's eventual diversification and expansion of services.

In the 1990s, the firm invested heavily in new computer technology and added resources positioning itself as a full-service accounting firm. From valuation services; mergers and acquisitions; tax planning and preparation; management advisory services; and auditing, review, and compilation services, Petty & Landis offers a comprehensive range of management and accounting services.

DEDICATED PROFESSIONALS

With an extraordinarily dedicated and talented group of people, Petty & Landis realizes that excellence and client service is more than an abstract concept. It is a tangible goal that drives the company to surpass industry standards. This deeply held commitment is ingrained into every one of the company's professionals. Much of the firm's success in attracting and retaining high-caliber people can be attributed to the company's long-standing policy of encouraging its professionals to take on increasing levels of responsibility and build strong relationships with clients, and encouraging continued professional growth.

Such commitment to its employees directly benefits the firm's clients. Clients know that the professionals working on their account thoroughly understand their business. Moreover, they can count on Petty & Landis to bring in and develop new talent to keep ideas fresh and sharply focused.

Experienced, responsible management; innovative ideas, solutions, and flexible systems; and above all, a dedication to client service—these are the hallmarks of excellence clients will find every day at Petty & Landis.

BUILDING THE BRIDGE BETWEEN PROVIDING INNOVATIVE BUSINESS SOLUTIONS AND CREATING STRONG PERSONAL RELATIONSHIPS, BASED ON TRUST WITH ITS CLIENTS, HAS BEEN THE BASIS FOR PETTY & LANDIS' SUCCESS FOR MORE THAN THREE DECADES.

© DOUG BARNETTE PHOTOGRAPHY

OVENANT COLLEGE AND CHATTANOOGA CELEBRATE 35 YEARS OF partnership in 1999. Surprisingly, the campus high up on Lookout Mountain is only 15 minutes from downtown. Covenant has provided a Christ-centered, liberal arts education to many of Chattanooga's most valued employees, managers, and executives. ✳ "It is refreshing to have Covenant College graduates working for us," says

Al Duke, president of SunTrust Bank of Chattanooga. "They have the ability to sift through overwhelming information, find the salient points for a decision, and act. My promise to other employers: Hire one Covenant graduate, and you will eventually hire another and another."

Covenant attracts dedicated students known for their academic ability from across the country and around the world. They hold the highest average SAT score of all top-tier Southern liberal arts colleges according to *U.S. News & World Report*'s 1998 college guide. More than 1,000 students pursue master's of education, bachelor's, associate's, or preprofessional degrees at Covenant. The college offers 18 major programs and six preprofessional programs. Covenant is accredited by the Southern Association of Colleges and Schools and is the college of the

THE HOTTEST YULETIDE TICKET IN CHATTANOOGA, COVENANT'S MADRIGAL DINNER IS A 30-YEAR CHATTANOOGA TRADITION. THE LORD AND LADY OF THE FEAST TOAST THEIR GUESTS (TOP).

COVENANT'S LOW STUDENT-TO-TEACHER RATIO ALLOWS PROFESSORS TO GET TO KNOW THEIR STUDENTS (BOTTOM).

Presbyterian Church in America (PCA).

Nearly 80 percent of Covenant's traditional teaching faculty have earned doctorates. They have received degrees from prominent institutions

including Yale, Harvard School of Business, Princeton, M.I.T., Notre Dame, and Virginia Polytechnic Institute. The student-to-teacher ratio is low, so professors get to know all their students and are available to them. "Students should not have to choose between an excellent education and a Christian education," President Frank Brock often says when describing Covenant's commitment to a strong academic program guided by the Reformed Christian faith.

"Covenant is one of Chattanooga's best-kept academic and economic secrets," Joseph Decosimo, senior partner of local accounting firm Joseph Decosimo and Company, says. More than 90 percent of Covenant's students receive financial aid. The college distributes more than $7 million in aid annually.

Covenant students train not only their minds but their hearts and hands as well, demonstrating Christ's love and power to reform individuals and societies. Covenant students tutor at-risk high schoolers, visit widows, lead inner-city sports clinics, and help in local shelters. The college requires all students to spend time in another culture to broaden their worldview as they experience the needs and opportunities of another country firsthand.

Through Covenant's Quest program, started in 1984, nearly 1,000 area adults have completed their bachelor's degrees at an accredited institution. These students receive the training they need to take on greater responsibility at work without interrupting their careers in the region's local businesses.

Covenant enhances the cultural life of Chattanooga through its well-established music department. Students and faculty are members of many church and community music organizations. The college's yearly

THE TOWER OF COVENANT'S CARTER HALL HAS BEEN A LOOKOUT MOUNTAIN LANDMARK FOR 70 YEARS.

Madrigal Dinner is "one of the hottest Yuletide tickets in the Chattanooga area," according to the *Chattanooga Free Press*. For 30 years, the college has prepared a traditional English Christmas feast for the community. The three-hour, eight-course meal is served by students in period costume while diners enjoy the Madrigal Choir and other entertainers. Covenant's dining room, the Tudor-style Great Hall, is a perfect setting for the celebration.

Covenant men and women compete intercollegiately (NAIA league, TVAC conference) in soccer, basket-ball, and cross-country. Women also compete in volleyball. Nationally ranked for the past five years, the Covenant men's soccer team was second only to Harvard and one of only seven teams in the nation to have a cumulative GPA over 3.0.

New buildings on campus meet the needs of growing enrollment. The C.G. and Nancy Mills Science Hall, completed in 1996, provides new labs, computer facilities, and classrooms. The Hugh O. Maclellen Sr. Residence Hall houses more than 180 students and provides areas for studying and socializing. The Martha Ashe Activities Center vastly expands the college's athletic facilities.

The tower of Covenant's Carter Hall atop Lookout Mountain can be seen by travelers from miles away. The 70-year-old building made several false starts as a grand Southern resort before becoming the center of Covenant College's campus. Much like the biblical saying that a city built upon a hill cannot be hid, Covenant and its 5,000 alumni strive to illumine Chattanooga and all the communities they enter with their motto, "In All Things . . . Christ Pre-eminent."

THE C.G. AND NANCY MILLS SCIENCE HALL, BUILT IN 1996, GREATLY EXPANDED THE COLLEGE'S SCIENCE FACILITIES.

Allied Arts of Greater Chattanooga

WHEN NEWCOMERS, VISITORS, OR LONGTIME RESIDENTS WANT to learn more about the cultural climate of the River City, Allied Arts of Greater Chattanooga is there to introduce them to the vibrant and varied forms of artistic expression flourishing here. The range of cultural activities and venues comprising the Chattanooga arts scene encompasses such

ALLIED ARTS OF GREATER CHATTANOOGA PROVIDES A UNITED VOICE FOR ALL CULTURAL ORGANIZATIONS AND ACTIVITIES IN HAMILTON COUNTY, STRIVES TO FURTHER THE SIGNIFICANCE OF THE ARTS IN THE COMMUNITY, OFFERS FINANCIAL ASSISTANCE TO STRENGTHEN THE AREA'S CULTURAL RESOURCES, AND WORKS WITH OTHER AGENCIES IN THE PUBLIC AND PRIVATE SECTOR TO MAKE QUALITY OF LIFE A PRIORITY ISSUE FOR THE COMMUNITY. ALLIED ARTS DOES NOT CREATE ART, BUT CREATES A CLIMATE IN WHICH THE ARTS CAN FLOURISH.

diverse mainstays as the Chattanooga Symphony and Opera, Bessie Smith Hall, Conference on Southern Literature, and Hunter Museum of American Art. All of these—and many more—receive financial support from Allied Arts.

In fact, for 30 years, Allied Arts has helped fuel and sustain much of the art and culture in Chattanooga. Examples of that patronage are easy to find. Visitors heading to downtown's Miller Plaza in spring or summer can catch a free Nightfall concert. Or they can visit the African American Museum, bring the kids to the Creative Discovery Museum, or explore the area's past at the Chattanooga Regional History Museum. Allied Arts supports a lengthy list of organizations each year.

To keep track of them all, Allied Arts publishes *Connections*, a bi-monthly calendar of events that showcases the area's ever changing cultural offerings. The publication is distributed free to more than 13,000 area households and businesses. In addition, Allied Arts' Artsline gives callers up-to-the-minute phone information about local art events, destinations, and festivals.

A UNIFIED VOICE FOR THE ARTS

Allied Arts provides a united voice for all cultural organizations and activities in Hamilton County, strives to further the significance of the arts in the community, offers financial assistance to strengthen the area's cultural resources, and works with other agencies in the public and private sector to make quality of life a priority issue for the community. Allied Arts does not create art, but creates a climate in which the arts can flourish.

Because the artistic urge often begins in school, Allied Arts is very involved in nurturing art-in-education programs. Allied Arts helps sponsor artists-in-residence programs that bring artists into the schools. Artists work hand in hand with teachers in local schools to enhance the curriculum and awaken the artist in each child. Additionally, schools and youth service organizations receive ongoing support to ensure that every child, regardless of ability to pay, can participate in cultural field trips all over Hamilton Country.

Of course, all these activities wouldn't be possible without generous help from area businesses and individuals. Nearly 85 percent of Allied Arts' annual funding comes from the private sector. Since its founding in 1969, Allied Arts has raised $30 million to help nurture the arts in Chattanooga. The effects of this fundraising are everywhere and are subtly evident throughout the city.

The arts have played a major role in Chattanooga's economic development, helping to spur the incredible downtown renaissance. By making Chattanooga a more attractive place to tourists, residents, and prospective newcomers, the arts have helped bring people back to the central city to live, work, and play. Additionally, the arts have helped residents understand their diversity and communicate in ways that cross racial, economic, and age barriers. And, of course, the arts have been good for the local economy, helping to directly employ more than 300 people—many more indirectly—and to increase the sales of goods and services offered by Chattanooga-area businesses.

Thanks to Allied Arts, Chattanooga's many cultural amenities will keep thriving—and, as a result, so will Chattanooga.

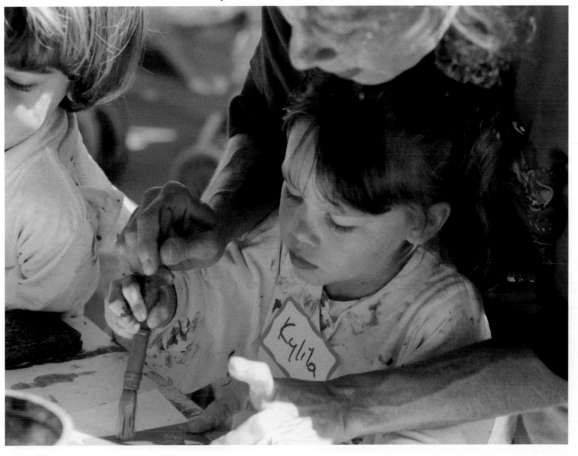

JUST "DECOSIMO" IS HOW THE CPA FIRM OF JOSEPH DECOSIMO AND Company, LLP is best known. But Decosimo can refer to Joe Decosimo, the man; his family; or the firm. ✳ Originally from Pennsylvania, Joseph F. Decosimo met and married Rachel Divine Sharp from Signal Mountain when they attended the University of Georgia. After graduate school at Northwestern University and

a short time in Chicago, they settled in Chattanooga in 1952 where Joe practiced as a CPA. He joined and became a partner of a local CPA firm. Then with partners Marion G. Fryar and Jerry V. Adams, he founded the Decosimo CPA firm on September 1, 1971.

The Decosimo CPA firm, ranked in 1996 and 1997 by the American Institute of CPAs as the 34th-largest CPA firm based on CPA membership, grew rapidly by providing a full line of financial services and working aggressively to help the firm's clients be successful. Most of the company's clients are families and family businesses. And most of the business clients are privately owned, although some are public companies, and Decosimo provides

guidance and services to businesses that go public.

Joe Decosimo says, "Our involvement with clients is more than purely financial. We feel a deep and abiding concern for our clients, and clients view us as trusted financial, business, and even personal advisers."

Four of Decosimo's nine children (Nick, Fred, Tom, and Rose) are CPAs with the firm, and some of his 25 grandchildren are expected to soon begin joining the practice. Even so, the firm is not made up just of Decosimo family members; there are about 20 other partners. The firm also has offices other than in Chattanooga and is affiliated worldwide through Jeffreys Henry International. The firm and its partners are members of numerous profes-

sional organizations, and recognized as leaders in the profession and the community. Much of what happens in Chattanooga, be it business, civic or social, has Decosimo members involved.

It is unlikely that the Decosimo firm will ever merge into the giant firms as many large CPA firms do. "Remaining an independent, regional firm and growing is more likely," states Managing Partner Jerry Adams, adding, "The financial gene is strong in the Decosimo family."

The Decosimo family of firms includes Decosimo Management Consulting, Decosimo Family Business Counselors, and Decosimo Conner Healthcare Financial Group, in addition to the Decosimo CPA firm.

CLOCKWISE FROM TOP LEFT: A PAINTING BY CHATTANOOGA ARTIST JIM WRIGHT PORTRAYS JOE DECOSIMO'S BUSINESS, CIVIC, AND PERSONAL LIFE.

JOINED BY THE MAYOR, GOVERNOR, AND COMPANY LEADERS, DECOSIMO (STANDING), CHAIRMAN OF PARTNERS FOR ECONOMIC PROGRESS, ANNOUNCES A NEW CHATTANOOGA MANUFACTURING PLANT.

HONORING CBMC PRESIDENT TED DEMOSS AT HIS RETIREMENT ARE BEN HADEN, JERRY ADAMS, JOE DECOSIMO, DEMOSS' GRANDDAUGHTER, AND SCOTTY PROBASCO.

TAPING A *Family Business Insight* TELEVISION PROGRAM ARE HOST JOE DECOSIMO (CENTER) WITH GUESTS WAYNE PETERS AND DECOSIMO PARTNER CHARLES HENDRY.

WITH ITS CONTINUED, MULTIMILLION-DOLLAR INVESTMENT IN NEW and renovated facilities and equipment, the Columbia/HCA Chattanooga Region is leading the way in making the highest quality of health care both convenient and affordable for citizens throughout the tristate region. Its family of facilities in the region includes four acute care hospitals, a freestanding psychiatric hospital, three urgent/emergency care centers, a fitness center, a freestanding surgery center, and a sports medicine facility.

Columbia/HCA hospitals in the tristate region include Parkridge Medical Center, East Ridge Hospital, and Valley Hospital, all in Chattanooga; Grandview Medical Center in Jasper; and Athens Regional Medical Center in Athens. Through this family of facilities, the Columbia/HCA system provides the region's most comprehensive network of services.

The organization's mission, adopted by each facility, leaves no doubt as to its employees' primary focus on the patient: "Above all else, we are committed to the care and improvement of human life. In recognition of this commitment, we will strive to deliver high-quality, cost-effective health care in the communities we serve."

ACCREDITED WITH COMMENDATION

While most other hospitals are accredited by the Joint Commission on Accreditation of Healthcare Organizations (JCAHO), all three of Columbia/HCA's Chattanooga facilities (East Ridge, Parkridge, and Valley) have earned Accreditation with Commendation, which is achieved by only 7 percent of hospitals nationwide. Also, Grandview Medical Center (formerly South Pittsburg Hospital) was named to the list of 100 Top Hospitals—Benchmarks for Success in 1998. Conducted annually by HCIA and Mercer's Health Care Provider Consulting practice, the study is designed to identify the U.S. hospitals delivering the most cost-efficient and highest-quality medical care.

The individual facilities of Columbia/HCA Chattanooga Region, whose presence in the area dates to 1971, boast a number of strengths and specialties. The system's flagship hospital, 296-bed Parkridge Medical Center, has established a reputation for excellence in cardiac care, orthopedics, sports medicine, and oncology, among other tertiary services, since its opening in 1971. A third Cardiac Catheterization Laboratory, dedicated to electrophysiology studies (mapping of the heart's electrical activity) opened recently. Its Diabetes Care Center and its Healthy Heart program provide outreach and education programs for citizens throughout the region. The Parkridge campus is home to four major medical office buildings, as well as the center for the region's most comprehensive Occupational Health Services program.

Parkridge's commitment to sports medicine is clearly evidenced in the comprehensive services provided through Chattanooga Sports Medicine (CSM)—formerly University Sports Medicine—serving the University of Tennessee at Chattanooga (UTC) and numerous high schools. A primary-care-based program that emphasizes the total care approach, CSM has the highest quality of orthopedic support and the finest physical therapy services in the region. Also, Parkridge's $1 million gift to UTC for development of a master's degree program in athletic training will benefit the community for decades to come.

East Ridge Hospital has, since its beginning in 1974, established a reputation for providing superior women's services. In addition to advanced laparoscopic surgical procedures, an 18-bed Neonatal Intensive Care Unit and the region's only Lactation Center complement the

PROVIDING A FULL RANGE OF SERVICES, EAST RIDGE HOSPITAL IS RECOGNIZED THROUGHOUT THE REGION FOR ITS SUPERIOR REPUTATION FOR OBSTETRICS AND NEONATAL INTENSIVE CARE SERVICES (TOP).

A REGIONAL MEDICAL CENTER, PARKRIDGE'S CAMPUS INCLUDES FOUR MAJOR MEDICAL OFFICE BUILDINGS AS WELL AS THE REGION'S CENTER FOR OCCUPATIONAL HEALTH SERVICES (BOTTOM).

facility's services for women. A $7.5 million expansion and renovation project substantially enlarged the Women's Center in 1998. A Breast Health Center is the latest addition. The facility provides a full range of services, including general and orthopedic surgery, and a newly expanded Emergency Care Center, with 16 treatment rooms. The hospital offers a growing number of specialty medical imaging sevices, including MRI.

The East Ridge Fitness Center, a 13,000-square-foot health and fitness center, is located directly behind the hospital. Personalized attention and individualized instruction are what make this fitness center different. An indoor swimming pool allows the center to offer unique programs such as Aqua Moms and Arthritis Water Therapy. Corporate membership packages are available.

Valley Hospital has served the tristate area for more than 20 years. Nestled amid 80 acres of woodland in the heart of Chattanooga, the 118-bed hospital provides unparalleled expertise in treating a broad range of behavioral health and chemical dependency problems. A talented, multidisciplinary team of mental health specialists, including psychiatrists, psychologists, psychiatric nurses, social workers, activity therapists, and counselors, carry out their mission of healing mental and behavioral illnesses. Valley offers the region's only inpatient, adult, Christian-based psychiatric treatment program, New Horizons, as well as a comprehensive geropsychiatric service, Senior Life Center. Valley's Child and Adolescent Services have been redesigned and refurbished to meet the needs of children and families.

In the fall of 1998, a new, $28 million, state-of the-art hospital opened to serve residents of the Sequatchie Valley. Grandview Medical Center is a prototype for new Columbia/ HCA hospitals of its size throughout the United States. The 50-bed facility replaced the 39-year-old hospital in South Pittsburg, and offers expanded and new services such as geriatrics and obstetrics.

Offering a full range of patient care, Columbia/HCA Chattanooga Region provides a complete continuum of services, whether it's a wellness program or outpatient surgery, open-heart surgery or obstetrics, occupational health or neonatal intensive care. The organization's strong belief in its mission to further the "care and improvement of human life"—along with its continued substantial investments in the tristate area—shows Columbia/HCA Chattanooga Region's unparalleled commitment to the community.

THE VALLEY HOSPITAL CAMPUS IS HOME TO THE TRISTATE REGION'S MOST COMPREHENSIVE RANGE OF BEHAVIORAL HEALTH AND CHEMICAL DEPENDENCY TREATMENT SERVICES FOR CHILDREN, ADOLESCENTS, ADULTS, AND SENIORS.

FROM THE FIRST MOMENTS OF LIFE THROUGH THE GOLDEN YEARS, THE COLUMBIA/HCA FAMILY OF FACILITIES IN THE CHATTANOOGA REGION PROVIDES A FULL RANGE OF SERVICES FOR INDIVIDUALS OF ALL AGES.

O VER THE YEARS, TELEVISION COMMERCIALS HAVE TOLD PEOPLE WHAT TO do when a package absolutely, positively has to get there overnight. ✳ But what if that package absolutely, positively has to get there today? Well, people in the Chattanooga area—and in hefty chunks of Georgia, Alabama, and the rest of Tennessee—call AAA Courier Service. Founded in 1975, AAA Courier Service has grown from a one-man operation to an 80-person company operating a fleet of vehicles out of three offices in Tennessee: Chattanooga, Knoxville, and Nashville. Through those offices, AAA Courier routinely handles thousands of shipments to points all over the United States, particularly in the East. Most often, those shipments are picked up and delivered the same day.

LIFE-SAVING SHIPMENTS

The company has made a name for itself through its timely, careful, and efficient handling of valuable—often irreplaceable— goods. AAA delivers human hearts, kidneys, and livers to surgeons performing transplants, and brings needed medicines to pharmacies from pharmaceutical company distribution centers. And AAA routinely transports critical payroll materials for its banking customers, as well as legal documents for law firms.

Such responsibility requires constant vigilance on the part of AAA employees. According to AAA owner Sid Brown, "Whether it's as precious as a heart for a transplant, as confidential as legal documents, as highly guarded as money, as fragile as computer equipment, as crucial as life saving medicine, as one-of-a-kind as a family's picnic photos, as light as a feather, or as heavy as an elephant, our AAA team is dedicated to providing our customers with top-priority service seven days a week, around the clock—no matter if it's a scheduled or special delivery/pickup."

MORE THAN CONVENIENCE

AAA Courier's same-day service offers more than simple convenience and timely delivery. One of Brown's banking customers estimates that using AAA's same-day turnaround has earned the bank an extra $120,000 per year in interest—money that would have been lost had the bank waited a mere 12 hours each day to make its deposit.

And that's just one bank. Many of AAA's largest customers entrust Brown's firm with transporting all the checks they receive. Those same-day deliveries translate into huge interest earnings for AAA's customers.

In addition to contributing to the earnings of its customers, AAA Courier Service has long been a contributor to Chattanooga causes. The firm has supported the construction of the University of Tennessee at Chattanooga's Finley Stadium, Allied Arts, and Hunter Museum, to name a few. With its quick, reliable delivery and commitment to the community, AAA Courier Service can truly say it has time for everyone.

ACCORDING TO AAA OWNER SID BROWN, "WHETHER IT'S AS PRECIOUS AS A HEART FOR A TRANSPLANT, AS CONFIDENTIAL AS LEGAL DOCUMENTS, AS HIGHLY GUARDED AS MONEY, AS FRAGILE AS COMPUTER EQUIPMENT, AS CRUCIAL AS LIFE SAVING MEDICINE, AS ONE-OF-A-KIND AS A FAMILY'S PICNIC PHOTOS, AS LIGHT AS A FEATHER, OR AS HEAVY AS AN ELEPHANT, OUR AAA TEAM IS DEDICATED TO PROVIDING OUR CUSTOMERS WITH TOP-PRIORITY SERVICE SEVEN DAYS A WEEK, AROUND THE CLOCK—NO MATTER IF IT'S A SCHEDULED OR SPECIAL DELIVERY/PICKUP."

MOUNTAIN CITY REALTORS IS THE EMBODIMENT OF A SMALL FIRM making a big impact on people's lives. The company, which has been active in the Chattanooga community since 1983 (with a brief hiatus in the early 1990s), is led by Lois Killebrew, a businessperson whose vision always rests squarely on the needs of her clients. As a result, she is among the most successful real estate professionals in the Chattanooga area.

Killebrew's list of qualifications and accomplishments is impressive. After earning her real estate license in 1971, she received her Certified Residential Broker (CRB) and Certified Residential Specialist (CRS) designations. Killebrew has been president of the Chattanooga Association of Realtors, served on the board of directors of the Chattanooga and Tennessee Associations of Realtors, and been regional vice president of the National Association of Realtors Women's Council and the Tennessee Association of Realtors. She currently serves on the board of directors of the Chattanooga Area Chamber of Commerce and is an active member of the Chattanooga-Hamilton County Regional Planning Commission. Killebrew has been instrumental in forming a Signal Mountain Chamber of Commerce and is currently serving as president.

FOCUSING ON CLIENTS' NEEDS

What really distinguishes Killebrew and her six-person staff is their sincere interest in helping the people they serve. To Mountain City Realtors, that means establishing genuine, one-on-one relationships with clients. Nowhere is that personalized approach more important than in Mountain City's relocation services, which account for 60 percent of the firm's business, with the rest devoted to residential and commercial real estate sales.

"Before we do anything else, we look at the unique needs of the family and each family member we're relocating," Killebrew explains. "We send them an information packet and questionnaire within 24 hours of our first conversation. The questionnaire helps us get to know the family and its members, and we use that information as a sounding board for further talks."

For example, if a family has adolescent children, Mountain City determines what types of activities they enjoy, what they like about their current school, and what their plans are for the future. Similarly, the firm finds out if younger children are involved in gymnastics, swimming, Scouts, or other extracurricular activities. Mountain City also inquires about the parents' leisure-time interests, the kind of home they like, and the style of living they're accustomed to. Once a client's needs are identified, Killebrew and her team can locate properties in the Greater Chattanooga area that best meet the requirements of the entire family.

"We go the extra mile throughout the relocation process," Killebrew adds. "We will set up hotel accommodations for the family, meet them at the airport, and make ourselves available during their visit—whatever our clients want us to do to help them find the right house. And with our Internet and E-mail capabilities, we can keep in close, quick contact with them no matter where they are."

Such personal attention to detail has served Mountain City's clients well. The firm has helped move families from as far away as Japan, South Africa, and Iran—not to mention countless locales across the United States. For a boutique-style real estate agency, Mountain City Realtors is one big example of how a small firm can successfully embrace today's global economy—and never lose the personal touch.

CLOCKWISE FROM TOP:
FOR A BOUTIQUE-STYLE REAL ESTATE AGENCY, MOUNTAIN CITY REALTORS IS ONE BIG EXAMPLE OF HOW A SMALL FIRM CAN SUCCESSFULLY EMBRACE TODAY'S GLOBAL ECONOMY—AND NEVER LOSE THE PERSONAL TOUCH.

MOUNTAIN CITY REALTORS, WHICH HAS BEEN ACTIVE IN THE CHATTANOOGA COMMUNITY SINCE 1983 (WITH A BRIEF HIATUS IN THE EARLY 1990S), IS LED BY LOIS KILLEBREW, A BUSINESSPERSON WHOSE VISION ALWAYS RESTS SQUARELY ON THE NEEDS OF HER CLIENTS.

NOWHERE IS THE PERSONALIZED APPROACH MORE IMPORTANT THAN IN MOUNTAIN CITY'S RELOCATION SERVICES, WHICH ACCOUNT FOR 60 PERCENT OF THE FIRM'S BUSINESS, WITH THE REST DEVOTED TO RESIDENTIAL AND COMMERCIAL REAL ESTATE SALES.

Volunteer Bank & Trust Company

SINCE VOLUNTEER BANK & TRUST COMPANY'S BEGINNINGS IN 1983, being Serious about Service has been the bank's primary emphasis. Volunteer Bank's mission—then and now—is to be the best bank in the neighborhoods it serves by focusing on better customer service, both personally and technologically, that is tailored to the specific needs of its consumer and business clients. Over the years, Volunteer Bank has proved that great service fuels growth, sustains earnings at levels that outperform peer group banks, and rewards its shareholders.

Volunteer Bank is a member of the Community Group, Inc., a six-bank holding company headquartered in Chattanooga, with banks located across Tennessee. To enable all Volunteer Bank associates to deliver the best possible bank and bank service to its clients, staff development and educational opportunities are vital at Volunteer Bank. The bank strongly believes that personal and professional growth leads to professional service—the level of service that differentiates Volunteer Bank from its competitors.

A GROWING BASE OF BUSINESS

More than 7,000 consumer and business customers make up Volunteer Bank's rapidly growing base. In addition to operating the Hixson and Shallowford Road offices, the bank completed renovation of the former Woolworth Store in downtown Chattanooga in 1996 and relocated the main office there. This renovation not only enhanced the ongoing revitalization of the downtown area but, more important, afforded Volunteer Bank's customers the best and most convenient banking facility in Hamilton County.

Based on its long-term success, Volunteer Bank believes that consumers and businesses in Hamilton County are looking for its brand of personal service. Over the next several years, the bank plans to open neighborhood banks in strategic locations throughout the region. However, the bank's vision includes more than just new neighborhood banks. Volunteer Bank plans to bring more convenience to its current and future customers with the use of the latest technologies. The company is examining opportunities for a network of cash dispensers and automated teller machines to be located separately from its full-service banking facilities. Touchtone telephone banking—which the bank is introducing—allows customers to check account balances, transfer balances between accounts, order a list of checks cleared since the last statement date, and perform other deposit account actions over the telephone.

SERVICE ALWAYS COMES FIRST

Be it automated or personally delivered, Volunteer Bank knows the importance of remaining dedicated to serious personal service throughout the bank. At other financial institutions, customers are too often treated like a number. At Volunteer Bank, customers are often friends and neighbors, and every customer is greeted cordially—usually by name.

Developing service relationships that endure over time has always been the foundation of Volunteer's success. A bank that acts small but delivers large, Volunteer Bank promises to be both friend and Serious about Service for years to come.

MANY CHATTANOOGANS HAVE EMBRACED 100.7 WUSY-FM "US-101" with a loyalty that underscores the station's slogan: Chattanooga's Hot Country Favorite. US-101's ratings speak for themselves. The station is the number-one-rated radio station in Chattanooga, having earned the highest audience share in two key population segments: listeners who are age 12 and older and adults who are 25 to 54 years old. Those numbers are particularly impressive in light of US-101's status as a relative newcomer to the community, having begun operations in Chattanooga in 1983.

"The success we've had at US-101 can be directly attributed to our very loyal listeners," says Market Manager Sammy George. "We truly appreciate the way our listeners have let us become part of their lives. There are a lot of radio stations for people to choose from in Chattanooga—we feel very fortunate that they've chosen US-101 and made us a household name in this exciting community."

The scope of the station's success extends well beyond the local area. US-101's huge following in the Chattanooga market has earned the station the distinction of having one of the largest audience shares in America—a standing that takes into account all markets and all radio stations, regardless of format.

WINNING AWARDS

Not surprisingly, perhaps, US-101 has been a finalist or has won every major national radio broadcasting award. Three years in a row—1995 through 1997—the station brought home the Country Music Association's highest honor: the Station of the Year Award. As might be expected, such recognition has not been limited to the station alone. David Hughes, US-101's afternoon air personality, received the prestigious Personality of the Year Award from the Country Music Association in 1994.

"One of our greatest strengths," explains George, "is the talented people we have on the air. Most of them have been with us for years, and they've built up loyal audiences that consider our personalities part of their family."

DOING THE RIGHT THING

For US-101, being part of the Chattanooga family is about more than great country music and top-rated on-air personalities. The station is deeply committed to public service and community involvement. For example, US-101 helped raise $1.2 million for Memphis-based St. Jude Children's Research Hospital in the eight years from 1991 to 1998, including $283,000 in 16 hours during the 1998 US-101/St. Jude Radiothon.

US-101 has also responded vigorously to local and regional disasters. In the past, the station has raised relief money for Gulf Coast and Carolina hurricane victims, and has started a special fund to help those Chattanooga residents whose homes were destroyed in a 1997 tornado. In 1998, US-101's commitment to community service was recognized by the National Association of Broadcasters with its prestigious Crystal Award.

On the lighter side, US-101 knows how to throw a great party. The station has brought some of the biggest names in country music to Chattanooga: Garth Brooks, Reba McEntire, and Brooks & Dunn, to name a few. When US-101 sponsored its 15th Anniversary Family Reunion, the all-day outdoor concert celebration saw a host of top country stars perform, including Lorrie Morgan, Ricochet, Clay Walker, John Berry, Keith Harling, Jo Dee Messina, and Michael Peterson.

With a bevy of broadcasting awards, top-notch on-air talent, and a deep concern for the community, US-101 is Chattanooga's Hot Country Favorite in more ways than one.

CLOCKWISE FROM TOP:
THE STATION HAS BROUGHT SOME OF THE BIGGEST NAMES IN COUNTRY MUSIC TO CHATTANOOGA. BROOKS & DUNN ARE PICTURED HERE WITH 1994 COUNTRY MUSIC ASSOCIATION PERSONALITY OF THE YEAR DAVID HUGHES (CENTER).

US-101 COLLECTED RELIEF ITEMS FOR THE VICTIMS OF A TORNADO THAT HIT CHATTANOOGA IN 1997. IN 1998, US-101'S COMMITMENT TO COMMUNITY SERVICE WAS RECOGNIZED BY THE NATIONAL ASSOCIATION OF BROADCASTERS WITH ITS PRESTIGIOUS CRYSTAL AWARD.

US-101 IS DEEPLY COMMITTED TO PUBLIC SERVICE AND COMMUNITY INVOLVEMENT.

I N LITTLE MORE THAN A DECADE, U.S. XPRESS ENTERPRISES HAS GROWN TO become Tennessee's largest trucking company and one of the largest publicly owned companies in Chattanooga. The reason, according to Co-chairman Patrick Quinn, is simple: "We're a different kind of trucking company." ✳ To understand the phenomenal growth of U.S. Xpress, one has to throw out any preconceived and antiquated notions of what a

trucking company is. This firm is literally transforming the industry through a customer-responsive paradigm that unites service, technology, and geographical coverage in ways never before thought possible.

JUST-IN-TIME SERVICE

In the early 1980s, the concept of just-in-time manufacturing and distribution was introduced to American industry. In simple terms, the concept calls for a more fluid production and distribution process, whereby raw materials, components, and finished goods are in continual movement within the manufacturing cycle. Materials are moved in a constant

flow, with neither too many nor too few, but always just enough and just in time—thus eliminating huge inventories and expensive warehouses.

U.S. Xpress was the first trucking company to offer the type of service the new process demanded, delivering freight with incredible speed and reliability. Incredible because in 1985, when U.S. Xpress entered the market, the concept of moving freight across the country in one or two days—as U.S. Xpress promised—was virtually unheard of. Still bogged down by the lingering effects of previous government regulation, other trucking companies typically delivered freight using very imprecise

schedules that could vary from several hours to a few days.

In addition, U.S. Xpress promised to move freight across the country in two days, whereas most typical trucking companies required a week or more for cross-country service. U.S. Xpress delivered on its promise of fast, reliable, expedited service. The company put two drivers in many of its tractors in order to make expedited deliveries. Coupled with the firm's heavy investment in training, equipment, and technology, the team-driven rigs turned U.S. Xpress trailers into virtual rolling warehouses.

TECHNOLOGY: THE DRIVING FORCE

Technology continues to be one of the prime reasons for the success of U.S. Xpress. Through the use of technological innovations, the company guarantees time-definite service, streamlines communications with customers, and enhances safety.

To achieve delivery speed and reliability, U.S. Xpress has equipped all tractors with real-time mobile satellite communications. As a result, the company knows where each truck is at all times, can tell if shipments are falling behind schedule due to traffic or bad weather, and can suggest alternate routes. U.S. Xpress can also give drivers customer orders; loading instructions; and fuel, mileage, payroll, safety, and maintenance information. Additionally, the company's computer tracks all 4,000 of its trucks and routes at once, and offers the optimized way for each delivery to be made.

According to Co-chairman Max Fuller, "Our computer system can analyze the data for each delivery by specific criteria: which combination of driver or drivers, route, and load will produce the fastest service to our customer; which combination will offer the lowest cost; and which alternative will bring the driver home in a timely way. Our operations

U.S. XPRESS' CUSTOMERS CAN OBTAIN REAL-TIME INFORMATION ON THEIR SHIPMENTS THROUGH THE COMPANY'S INTERNET WEB SITE USING XPRESS CONNECT™.

people can weigh those alternatives against the priorities the delivery requires and can make fast, well-informed decisions."

INTEGRATED TECHNOLOGIES STREAMLINE COMMUNICATIONS

U.S. Xpress has integrated its delivery-oriented technologies with others that serve the company's interactions with customers, thereby greatly improving the efficiency and responsiveness of communications. Through Electronic Commerce, customers can tender loads, trace shipments, generate scanned bills of lading, receive and pay invoices, and produce reports. Xpress Connect™, the company's proprietary Internet solution, provides a lower-cost alternative to traditional electronic data interchange methods, allowing customers to access the company's Web site to exchange more information with greater flexibility.

U.S. Xpress' technology focuses on safety, too. "Driving safely is the most important thing our drivers do," says Fuller. "We have invested heavily in technology, training, and equipment to prevent accidents. In the final analysis, though, our success is due to the dedication and commitment of our drivers to be good citizens of the road at all times."

For example, the company has equipped all of its Freightliner Century Class tractors with Eaton VORAD, a radar-based collision avoidance system that alerts drivers to traffic around them, letting drivers "see" into the blind spots that are often the sources of accidents. U.S. Xpress was also the first trucking company to install antilock brakes on all its tractors—long before the government mandated their use.

U.S. Xpress' drivers undergo training prior to employment and participate in ongoing safety refresher courses. Driver education includes vehicle-specific training, defensive driving techniques, and professional driver ethics.

COVERING MORE TERRITORY

While most trucking companies are regionally focused, U.S. Xpress provides a range of services over the entire geographic area it

TWENTY-FIVE PERCENT OF U.S. XPRESS' DRIVERS ARE FEMALE (TOP).

COUPLED WITH THE FIRM'S HEAVY INVESTMENT IN TRAINING, EQUIPMENT, AND TECHNOLOGY, THE TEAM-DRIVEN RIGS HAVE TURNED U.S. XPRESS TRAILERS INTO VIRTUAL ROLLING WAREHOUSES (BOTTOM).

covers. U.S. Xpress provides, for example, expedited service to any point in the 48 contiguous states and Canada. Regional services are offered in the southeastern, midwestern, and western regions of the United States. The company also has a full-service logistics group that specializes in serving the air freight industry.

With a growth rate exceeding 20 percent throughout the 1990s, a rapidly expanding workforce that already totals more than 7,000, and an aggressive approach to acquisitions, U.S. Xpress promises to be a leader in the Chattanooga area—and far beyond—for years to come.

Chattanooga Neighborhood Enterprise, Inc.

MORE THAN 10 YEARS AGO, LEADERS FROM THE CITY OF CHATTANOOGA and Hamilton County, the Lyndhurst Foundation, and a number of local banks, private citizens, and corporations joined efforts to address Chattanooga's growing inner-city housing and neighborhood development needs. At a time when many of the community's older residential areas were experiencing a decline in home

ownership and housing in general showed increasing signs of neglect, the goal was to dramatically improve existing housing, develop new housing, and generally revitalize inner-city neighborhoods.

Created in 1986, Chattanooga Neighborhood Enterprise, Inc. (CNE) is a private, nonprofit corporation founded to lead the city's public-private housing initiative. Its mission is to provide the opportunity for all Chattanoogans to live in fit, decent, and affordable housing. When the organization came into existence, only about $1.2 million was available annually for low-income housing activity in Chattanooga. The CNE partnership effort now generates almost 20 times that amount.

While 1997 saw a number of successful innovations and noteworthy achievements for Chattanooga Neighborhood Enterprise, the year also marked a significant milestone for the organization itself—CNE celebrated its 10th anniversary. After a decade of serving Chattanooga's housing needs, the organization's mission has never been clearer.

"Our primary objective will always be centered on providing affordable housing for all Chattanooga residents. But we also believe in a greater mission of community building, including initiatives that create diverse, mixed-income neighborhoods and serve as examples for downtown housing programs," says Leigh Ferguson, president of CNE. "Building houses is not enough. We try to build neighborhoods where we'd all like to live."

SIGNIFICANT COMMUNITY INVESTMENT

Since its inception, CNE has helped create, finance, or rehabilitate more than 4,500 units of affordable housing in Chattanooga, representing an investment of more than $135 million. By developing a

mix of affordable housing (restricted to people with moderate incomes) and market-rate housing (which carries no income restrictions), CNE aims to show private developers how broad the downtown housing market can become.

To see its mission through, CNE has divided its efforts into six main businesses: home improvement, home purchase, affordable rental, housing development, home buyer education, and technical assistance to community developers.

The organization's expertise has been recognized across the country, and CNE is committed to providing

both training and incentive for families whose goal is home ownership or rehabilitation. Likewise, CNE offers various types of technical assistance to a number of local housing organizations and to qualified owners for the improvement of their homes, as well as for repairs needed to eliminate emergency or life-threatening conditions.

As Chattanooga Neighborhood Enterprise looks to the future, consistently broadening and reshaping its focus, its mission remains the same—to provide the opportunity for all Chattanoogans to live in fit, decent, and affordable housing.

AFTER RENTING FOR MANY YEARS, CAROLYN, NICHOLAS, AND ROBERT PERRY RECENTLY PURCHASED THEIR OWN HOME BY WORKING CLOSELY WITH CHATTANOOGA NEIGHBORHOOD ENTERPRISE.

CNE HAS HELPED MANY NEIGHBORHOODS RETURN TO THEIR ORIGINAL STATE, ALLOWING FAMILIES TO ENJOY A SAFE AND SECURE LIFESTYLE IN DOWNTOWN CHATTANOOGA.

THERE'S AN OLD SAYING THAT THE GREATEST SUCCESS IS OFTEN ACHIEVED by people who didn't realize they were trying the impossible. This holds true for Michael Walden, president and owner of Metropolitan Security, Inc. and the Chattanooga Small Business Council's 1997 Businessperson of the Year. ✳ Metropolitan was born in a spur-of-the-moment offer that changed Walden's life. An officer with the

Chattanooga Police Department, he had been supplementing his income by offering local businesses nighttime patrols. In 1990, one of Walden's customers asked him to help with the supervision of a 24-hour security firm it was planning to hire. With the determination that has characterized his business since that day, Walden offered to supply the security officers himself. It was a near impossible undertaking for the 26-year-old former navy search-and-rescue swimmer: There were already 22 security companies in the Chattanooga area.

Using his experience as a police officer and as a navy recruit company commander and instructor, Walden jumped in with both feet. Although he still had much to learn about obtaining the capital necessary to start a labor-intensive business, Walden was certain that a tough commitment to high-quality security officers and business integrity would keep the company alive.

It did, but as most business owners know, it is cash flow that can make or break a company. To ensure that he could meet payroll and pay bills, Walden went straight to his customers. Most were so pleased with Metropolitan's service, they agreed to a two-week billing cycle instead of the customary 30 days. Some even started paying as much as six months in advance. Walden and his wife, Amy—the company's CFO—also sold their cars and took a second mortgage on their house to further make ends meet.

Thanks to phenomenal client support, unrelenting determination, and Walden's gift for marketing, Metropolitan became the largest locally owned contract security service in the Chattanooga area and the third-largest privately held firm in the state of Tennessee. Today, Walden has more than 500 employees and has opened fully staffed branches in

Tennessee, Mississippi, and Georgia. Revenues for 1997 exceeded $5 million and Walden is predicting $10 million by 2000. His army of security officers sport highly recognizable uniforms and drive fully equipped patrol vehicles.

Metropolitan's success has earned Walden many awards. He is a graduate of Leadership Chattanooga and, in 1997, was elected to serve as president of the North Chattanooga Chamber of Commerce. He received the statewide Blue Chip Enterprise Initiative award from the U.S. Chamber of Commerce and Mass Mutual in 1997, and recently won the Tennessee Better Business Bureau's Torch Award for Marketplace Ethics in the 100-to-999 employees category. Also in 1997, Walden completed construction of a new corporate headquarters. In 1998, he received the Sam Walton Business Leader Award.

But Walden is not resting on his laurels; he is initiating a growth plan that envisions Walden Security— as the entire company will soon be known—in cities all across the state. He also plans to open offices in

other southeastern markets, such as Birmingham and Atlanta. With this aggressive growth, Walden estimates his company will have 1,000 employees by the year 2000.

Above all else, though, it is Walden's commitment to quality and integrity that has helped to make Metropolitan Security an invaluable partner to many of its customers. That partnership has made possible what most people would have thought couldn't be done.

MICHAEL WALDEN'S COMMITMENT TO QUALITY AND INTEGRITY HAS HELPED TO MAKE METROPOLITAN SECURITY, INC. AN INVALUABLE PARTNER TO MANY OF ITS CUSTOMERS.

THERE'S AN OLD SAYING THAT THE GREATEST SUCCESS IS OFTEN ACHIEVED BY PEOPLE WHO DIDN'T REALIZE THEY WERE TRYING THE IMPOSSIBLE. THIS HOLDS TRUE FOR WALDEN, PRESIDENT AND OWNER OF METROPOLITAN SECURITY AND THE CHATTANOOGA SMALL BUSINESS COUNCIL'S 1997 BUSINESSPERSON OF THE YEAR.

Ballet Tennessee
Baker-Van Cura Ballet Centre

"W E ARE CREATING LIFE SKILLS, SETTING THE STAGE FOR OUR students to realize their full potential, both in their own lives and in the community." So say Barry Van Cura and Anna Baker-Van Cura, the husband-and-wife team who founded Chattanooga's Ballet Tennessee and its complementary school, the Baker-Van Cura Ballet Centre, in 1987. "Dance is about discovering yourself. Teaching dance is helping people take that journey. It's something we do by providing a protective, nurturing environment within the traditional disciplines of classical ballet," say the Van Curas.

Such deep commitment to the personal development of their students may be one reason why Ballet Tennessee was tapped by the City of Chattanooga to bring dance to all its children. Ballet Tennessee works closely with the Chattanooga Parks and Recreation Department's Cultural Section to provide dance programs for the inner city.

Two initiatives that Ballet Tennessee helped to begin are the Talent Identification Program (TIP) and the Dance Alive summer program. Both were piloted in 1997 to reach and provide quality training to children from inner-city and rural areas. Both programs work in tandem with the company's outreach and educational projects to serve thousands of children annually.

A WINNING WAY WITH STUDENTS

Another reason the city called upon Ballet Tennessee could well be the ballet's many success stories. Company-trained students have danced with the San Francisco Ballet, Ballet West, Chicago City Ballet, American Ballet Theatre II, Pacific Northwest Ballet, Ohio Ballet, Joel Hall Dancers, and Twyla Tharp Company. Baker-Van Cura Ballet Centre students have been chosen for various university and summer workshops, including the Kirov Academy of Ballet in Washington, D.C., Alabama School of Fine Arts, North Carolina School of Arts, Interlochen Arts Academy, and Barat College in Chicago.

Ballet Tennessee has won numerous awards. Barry Van Cura's choreography, for example, has been cited three times at the PANOPLY Choreography Competition in Alabama, and his *Pocahontas* won first place

CLOCKWISE FROM TOP LEFT: *Pocahontas*, BALLET TENNESSEE'S FIRST-PLACE WINNER IN THE PANOPLY CHOREOGRAPHY COMPETITION, INCLUDES AS CAST MEMBERS LAUREL SHASTRI, JUSTIN BOLINGER, J.C. SHUMAKER, ERIC RUDOLPH, AND TIM MURPHY.

ANNA AND BARRY VAN CURA, WHO FOUNDED BALLET TENNESSEE AND THE BAKER-VAN CURA BALLET CENTRE IN 1987, PERFORM A SCENE FROM *Firebird*.

CHILDREN OF ALL AGES DELIGHT IN THE BAKER-VAN CURA BALLET'S STAGING OF *Alice in Wonderland*, FEATURING SUE ANNE WELLS AND DAVID PENNEBAKER.

BOB NICHOLS

ALAN VANDERGRIFF

in 1998. *Amethyst*, a 1995 University of Tennessee at Chattanooga collaboration shown nationally on Public Television, won an arts award in South Carolina and commendation in New York. Anna Baker-Van Cura has received two Outstanding Teacher Awards from the Tennessee Governor's School for the Arts. The award honors teachers who have been nominated by students for having a very positive influence on the students' lives.

YEARS OF EXPERIENCE

Barry and Anna Van Cura bring their years of professionalism and experience to their company and the training of dancers. Anna was selected by Frederic Franklin for a Ford Foundation Scholarship with the National Ballet of Washington, D.C. She rose to ballerina status through the ranks of the corps de ballet by dancing with Ruth Page's International Ballet. Other credits include American Ballet Theater, Chicago Ballet, Chicago Lyric Opera, and Cincinnati Opera. She was on the faculty of the University of Illinois-Urbana, Ruth Page Foundation, and Hubbard Street Dance Company. Anna served two terms as a panelist on the Ohio Arts Council and was recognized as an Artist in Education. She remains an out-of-state consultant for the council. Anna studied the Soviet method of ballet training in Russia, and was a master teacher at Bill Evans Summer Dance Institute, Northwest Florida Ballet, Tennessee Association of Dance, and Memphis Dance Alliance.

Barry has a bachelor of fine arts degree in ballet from North Carolina School of the Arts. He was selected by David Howard to apprentice at New York's Harkness Ballet. He danced with the Eglevsky Ballet, Chicago Ballet, Chicago Lyric Opera, Milwaukee Ballet, and Indianapolis Ballet Theater. Barry has choreographed opera and musical theater, as well as classical and contemporary ballet. He taught at Columbia College in Chicago and Ohio's Youngstown University. The Van Curas were directors of the National Academy of Dance, a community and high school boarding program in Champaign, Illinois. They founded and directed Chicago's Ballet Midwest.

AN EXCITING REPERTOIRE

Barry and Anna Van Cura's original programming of works gives the community a view of its heritage: *Earth's Heart* (about the Trail of Tears), *Ballet Goes Country*, *Tennessee Homecoming Tribute*, and *Bessie Smith Blues*. They restage the classics: *Cinderella*, *The Nutcracker*, *Swan Lake*, *Coppelia*, and *Firebird*. They reach to new audiences with *Dracula*, *Peter and the Wolf*, *Alice in Wonderland*, *A Christmas Carol*, and *Pocahontas*. The Van Curas stretch the limits of the dancers' technique and performance with new and contemporary choreography.

For many young dancers, Baker-Van Cura Ballet Centre has been a springboard to Ballet Tennessee.

Ballet Centre offers an intensive training program for talented and committed dancers, preparing them for professional careers. The school's mission is to develop a strong classical ballet technique and to offer quality training in related dance idioms. The progress of all students is graded to ensure a systematic development of muscles, technique, musicality, and performance.

With such a strong commitment to its students, its art, and its community, there's little wonder Ballet Tennessee and Baker-Van Cura Ballet Centre have so much of Chattanooga dancing.

CLOCKWISE FROM TOP LEFT: BARRY VAN CURA PORTRAYS THE INFAMOUS SCROOGE IN A RESTAGING OF CHARLES DICKENS' CLASSIC *A Christmas Carol*.

THE HUSBAND-AND-WIFE TEAM REACHES TO NEW AUDIENCES WITH ORIGINAL PROGRAMMING THAT INCLUDES *Dracula*.

BARRY AND ANNA VAN CURA ALSO RESTAGE CLASSICS SUCH AS *The Nutcracker*.

Chattanooga Choo-Choo
Holiday Inn

I N 1909, THE ORIGINAL TERMINAL STATION OPENED IN CHATTANOOGA TO welcome travelers and was hailed as the Gateway to the City. Today, restored and converted to the Chattanooga Choo-Choo Holiday Inn, the site is not only a station, but a destination that hosts nearly 1 million visitors a year. ☀ More than $8 million in renovations have been made since 1989—when the station was saved from the wrecking ball—to

restore the facility to its former elegance. An 85-foot-tall, freestanding dome now airily welcomes guests into the lavish lobby of the Chattanooga Choo-Choo Holiday Inn, where visitors can rest in the comfortable sitting area and marvel at the beautifully renovated Victorian architecture. Just outside, an exciting mix of shops, lush gardens, fine restaurants, and outstanding meeting facilities await business or vacation travelers.

The original Terminal Station operated until August 11, 1970, when the last train pulled away. In its heyday, nearly all trains heading south passed through Chattanooga, making it one of the most visited terminals in the Southeast. In fact, it even inspired the song made famous by the Glenn Miller Orchestra. Currently, guests can experience for themselves the charm of those bygone days through the painstakingly renovated appointments of yesteryear that make the Choo-Choo such a memorable and unique place to stay or visit.

SOMETHING
FOR EVERYONE

Guests and visitors can still stroll outside along the vintage tracks and train cars, walking among turn-

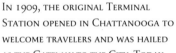

CLOCKWISE FROM TOP:
IN 1909, THE ORIGINAL TERMINAL STATION OPENED IN CHATTANOOGA TO WELCOME TRAVELERS AND WAS HAILED AS THE GATEWAY TO THE CITY. TODAY, RESTORED AND CONVERTED TO THE CHATTANOOGA CHOO-CHOO HOLIDAY INN, THE SITE IS NOT ONLY A STATION, BUT A DESTINATION THAT HOSTS NEARLY 1 MILLION VISITORS A YEAR.

AN 85-FOOT-TALL, FREESTANDING DOME NOW AIRILY WELCOMES GUESTS INTO THE LAVISH LOBBY OF THE CHATTANOOGA CHOO-CHOO HOLIDAY INN, WHERE VISITORS CAN REST IN THE COMFORTABLE SITTING AREA AND MARVEL AT THE BEAUTIFULLY RENOVATED VICTORIAN ARCHITECTURE.

CHILDREN OF ALL AGES ENJOY THE CHATTANOOGA CHOO-CHOO HOLIDAY INN.

of-the-century fountains and formal gardens where more than 500 dazzling varieties of roses grace the grounds. Equally mesmerizing are the sights and sounds from the carefully cultivated water garden, nestled among the flowering cherry trees, Japanese maples, and Elizabethan-style hedges. Many visitors let their olfactory sense guide them, drawing them to the Candy Factory to sample some homemade fudge and other delectable edibles. Still others watch local artisans crafting their wares.

There is no shortage of things to do and see. Children of all ages

can enjoy a trolley ride around the 24-acre campus. Those with a flair for the dramatic can pose for a photograph dressed in yesteryear's togs or have their portrait drawn by an on-site artist. And those who have always harbored a secret dream of standing at the controls of an old-fashioned steam engine can climb aboard the Chattanooga Choo-Choo engine and get a firsthand view of an authentic, wood-burning engine car.

MEMORABLE
ACCOMMODATIONS

The Chattanooga Choo-Choo Holiday Inn delivers 360 first-class accommodations, including 48 authentic, onboard train car sleeping parlors. These parlors each occupy a half-car and are furnished with beautiful Victorian antique reproductions. In addition, three different freestanding buildings accommodate a range of generous room styles and package choices, including elegant suites.

Three well-appointed pools and two spa areas are available for guests. One is located under a four-story-high skylight dome, complete with a water slide that spills into its own waterfall for year-round aquatic en-

tertainment. The two outdoor pool areas are open for a long southern season and include a water slide and an island that houses a covered whirlpool.

But the Choo-Choo is more than a great place for the family to frolic and relax; it is also the destination for the finest formal and casual dining, with five fine restaurants to choose from. The Gardens Restaurant offers fine family dining in a lush, fountain-like atmosphere. Visitors who enjoy steaks and show tunes can visit the Station House, Chattanooga's only restaurant with a singing wait staff. Guests wanting to dress up and be pampered can expect an intimate atmosphere at Dinner in the Diner, where an evening of Victorian ambience and freshly prepared delicacies await the discerning eye and palate. For more casual dining, the Silver Diner serves up pizza and cool sodas, while the Choo-Choo Café Espresso

offers an array of gourmet coffee drinks and deli sandwiches.

Any meal is sweeter when topped off at the Sidetrack Ice Cream Shop, packed with a variety of hand-dipped flavors, frozen yogurt, and soft-serve ice cream (open seasonally). After a long day of taking in Chattanooga's many attractions or attending a business conference, the Victorian Lounge, just off the Grand Dome Lobby, graciously offers libations in a plush-carpeted area under polished brass chandeliers.

When it finally comes time to get down to business, visitors need look no farther than around the corner or across the tracks to the Centennial Convention Center. The Roosevelt Room (named for both Franklin and Teddy Roosevelt) is a versatile facility with a capacity for 250 people. The Imperial Ballroom can seat 450 and affords a luxurious setting—complete with chandeliers and elegant

decor—for business or social functions. The Finley Lecture Hall is known for its comfort and functionality, and has become a top choice for first-class meeting space. And the Centennial Theater offers seating for 550 people, making it ideal for larger audio-visual presentations. There are other adaptable meeting rooms available for corporate and convention needs that offer more than 30,000 square feet of meeting space.

For business or pleasure, guests will find what they need at the Chattanooga Choo-Choo Holiday Inn. The grounds and amenities have changed quite a bit over the years, but the focus on hospitality and southern charm has not changed. Year after year, more and more visitors are finding that the most memorable ending to any Chattanooga vacation is also where it should begin—at the Chattanooga Choo-Choo Holiday Inn.

A T THE TURN OF THE CENTURY, AS THE TENNESSEE RIVER AND CHATTAnooga continued to attract wealth and industry, many of the families on the forefront of those ambitions built their lives and raised their children in a neighborhood known as Bluff View. Today, while their families' legacies live on in other Chattanooga landmarks, the neighborhood they once called home thrives as the Bluff View Art District.

Fueled perhaps by the same entrepreneurial spirit of the original resident "cliff dwellers," the Art District's cornerstone was established in 1991, when Dr. Charles and Mary Portera bought the former Newell House on the corner of High Street and East Second Street. The first of many investments the couple has made in the area, the District has become an award-winning example of sustainable urban renewal and preservation excellence—a place where the past meets the present to create a lively, sophisticated ambience perfect for meeting, dining, an overnight getaway, or enjoying the fine arts.

A commitment to reinvigorate this once elegant neighborhood into an area that would tantalize all of the human senses through art, architecture, scenic views, landscape, and food has continued without pause since 1991. Featured in *Southern Living*, *Country Living*, and *Country Inns* magazines, the District now offers the city's finest bed-and-breakfast

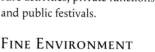

BLUFF VIEW ART DISTRICT IS RAPIDLY BECOMING A LEGACY FOR CHATTANOOGA, A CONTINUANCE OF THE RICH HISTORY THAT HAS ALWAYS MARKED THIS SPECIAL NEIGHBORHOOD (TOP).

RENAISSANCE COMMONS CONFERENCE CENTER PROVIDES AN OUTSTANDING BACKDROP FOR EXECUTIVE RETREATS, PRIVATE GATHERINGS, AND THE DISTRICT'S ELABORATE CULINARY SALUTES.

accommodations in three turn-of-the-century homes, an internationally acclaimed outdoor sculpture garden, a banquet and conference center, four restaurants, a fine-art gallery, and a bocce ball court and terrace.

Directly on the riverfront and conveniently connected to downtown's major attractions and central business district via the Tennessee Riverwalk and Walnut Street Pedestrian Bridge, Bluff View Art District has become

the premier destination for cultural and culinary arts, business and leisure activities, private functions, and public festivals.

FINE ENVIRONMENT FOR BUSINESS

I n the center of the District is the District's center for business: Renaissance Commons. Offering exquisite architecture, sophisticated meeting spaces, fine cuisine, and exceptional service, Renaissance Commons is outstanding. For elegant and intimate dinners or board meetings and seminars, the selection of private rooms provides diverse amenities to suit form and function. Accenting each of the rooms are select pieces from the District's permanent art collection, as well as exotic and antique woods custom crafted into cabinetry, functional centerpieces, and media centers. The renowned staff of professional chefs orchestrate menus for conferences and events from morning breaks to inventive seven-course dinners. This impressive and productive environment reflects the overall commitment to excellence resounding throughout the Art District. Combined with fine accommodations and additional meeting space at the District's bed and breakfast, Bluff View Inn, these one-stop amenities have positioned the area as a premier destination for executive retreats.

ROOMS WITH A VIEW AT BLUFF VIEW INN

Wrapped around the historic neighborhood are three restored, architecturally diverse homes that comprise the Bluff View Inn. Offering a total of 16 guest rooms, the Inn provides amenities unmatched in the downtown area. Individual homes and the guest rooms within are each named for Chattanooga residents, prominent citizens, and families who made their homes on the bluff. A tour of rooms is a living history of Chattanooga's exciting story. In 1993, the C.G. Martin House was the first home to be renovated and opened as Bluff View Inn. The T.C. Thompson House, a Victorian-style home built in 1908, was next to become part of Bluff View Inn, in 1994. Opened in May of 1997, Bluff View Inn's Maclellan House sits on the bluff's crest overlooking the Tennessee River. In this handsomely restored English Tudor, Inn guests enjoy a gourmet break-

fast in the Audubon Room, with a picture-window view of the river. The new bocce court and terrace next to the Maclellan House provide a relaxing option to guests looking for nearby activities.

A CELEBRATION OF CULINARY ARTS

Applauded year-round for inventive menus, elaborate culinary salutes, and signature specialty pastas, breads, French pastries, and chocolates, the Bluff View Art District has evolved into a cutting-edge culinary district as well. Four separate restaurants with terrace seating, river views, and colorful atmospheres are connected by landscaped alleys and pathways, creating a dining-out experience reminiscent of a small European village. Back Inn Cafe is the District's Italian bistro, with a changing menu served in the colonial-revival Martin House mansion overlooking the Tennessee River and Sculpture Garden. Tony's Pasta Shop and Trattoria, in the carriage house of the T.C. Thompson House, features the District's popular house-made pastas, sauces, and breads. Rembrandt's Coffee House features the talents of the District's French pastry chef and chocolatier, as well as fresh salads, sandwiches, soups, fresh roasted gourmet coffees, teas, and accessories. Renaissance Commons serves an elegant Sunday brunch buffet in the magnificent River Room. Gathering at the Commons during the holidays for exquisite dinners has become a tradition now for many families.

THE WORLD COMES TO THE BLUFF VIEW ART DISTRICT

A visit to the Art District can seem like a passport to culinary and artistic pursuits from around the globe. River Gallery Sculpture Garden has been selected by the International Sculpture Center for inclusion in its *Sculpture Parks and Gardens Directory*. On permanent exhibit in the garden are the Wuxi Rocks, given to the City of Chattanooga from the sister city of Wuxi, China. Changing monthly exhibits, art festivals, and other fine collections inside River Gallery feature the works of more than 300 artists

from around the country. An annual Russian and Ukrainian art exhibit now includes an opening-weekend four-course Russian dinner, prepared and presented by the executive chef. Other culinary salutes have included a five-course Japanese dinner, a tribute to history's greatest chefs, and special menus created to complement current and traveling art exhibits sponsored by the River Gallery and the neighboring Hunter Museum of American Art. The District's team of chefs all come together to create authentic selections for the popular annual Oktoberfest event, held over two days in October. A walk through the District's coffee house will leave you with a taste of France, while lunch or dinner at Tony's Pasta Shop provides a taste of old Italy; and Back Inn Cafe's contemporary Italian menu takes an adventurous turn through California.

The Bluff View Art District has become more than a trendy destination. It is rapidly becoming a legacy for Chattanooga, a continuance of the rich history that has always marked this special neighborhood.

CLOCKWISE FROM TOP LEFT: BACK INN CAFE IS ONE OF FOUR UNIQUE RESTAURANTS IN THE ART DISTRICT. THE CHANGING MENUS FEATURE THE TALENTS OF A TEAM OF PROFESSIONAL CHEFS FROM CULINARY INSTITUTIONS ALL ACROSS THE COUNTRY.

GUESTS OF BLUFF VIEW INN CAN CHOOSE TO ENJOY COMPLIMENTARY BREAKFAST ON THE TERRACE AT REMBRANDT'S COFFEE HOUSE.

THE INTERNATIONALLY ACCLAIMED RIVER GALLERY SCULPTURE GARDEN FEATURES A NEW EXHIBIT EACH YEAR.

RIVER GALLERY REPRESENTS MORE THAN 300 ARTISTS AND FINE CRAFTSMEN FROM ACROSS THE COUNTRY.

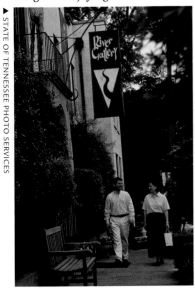

THE TENNESSEE AQUARIUM, WHICH OPENED IN CHATTANOOGA IN THE spring of 1992, is the world's first major institution dedicated to freshwater ecosystems. Focusing primarily on the Tennessee River and related systems, the aquarium's exhibits are organized to guide visitors on a journey from the river's source in the Appalachian high country, through its midstream, and finally to the Mississippi Delta.

Visitors leave the Tennessee Aquarium with an appreciation of how the natural world is tied together through moving water.

Founded as a private, nonprofit, educational organization, and owned by the Tennessee Aquarium Corporation, the aquarium is dedicated to the understanding, conservation, and enjoyment of rivers. In total, the 12-story, 130,000-square-foot building holds more than 400,000 gallons of water in its 50 exhibits. It is home to more than 9,000 animals, including 400 species of fish, birds, mammals, reptiles, and amphibians. The aquarium also houses a 200-seat auditorium, two fully equipped classrooms, and a wet lab.

Across the street from the Tennessee Aquarium, an IMAX® 3D Theater with a six-story screen invites viewers into an engulfing world where up to 400 people at a time can intimately experience realistic 3-D wizardry. Because of its technologically advanced 3-D cameras, rolling-loop projector, special polarized glasses, and large-format film, children and adults alike find themselves exploring places they never thought possible.

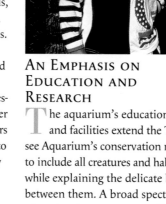

RICHARD T. BRYANT

An Emphasis on Education and Research

The aquarium's education staff and facilities extend the Tennessee Aquarium's conservation mission to include all creatures and habitats, while explaining the delicate balance between them. A broad spectrum of educational programs are offered to students of all ages—in organized groups, in member programs, and in one-on-one encounters.

Each year, hundreds of teachers from Tennessee, Georgia, and Alabama come to the aquarium to enhance their knowledge, teaching skills, and effectiveness as environmental education leaders in their schools. Awakening and exciting teachers about the environment creates a ripple effect far beyond the doors of the aquarium. This synergy springboards from workshops developed by aquarium educators, which are taught to teachers, who in turn relay the environmental message to their students.

The Environmental Learning Lab at the IMAX Center reaches classrooms everywhere through videoconferencing. Schools linked to the Internet interact with aquarium educators, scientists, and with each other as they raise questions, explore environmental issues, and learn about the natural world.

RICHARD T. BRYANT

The aquarium also has a strong interest in aquatic research. The Southeast Aquatic Research Institute (SARI) is a nonprofit organization formed by the Tennessee Aquarium, the University of Tennessee at Chattanooga, and the Tennessee River Gorge Trust to protect the region's natural resources through scientific research, training of environmental professionals, education of the public, conservation of natural resources, and encouragement of young scientific leaders.

Through these efforts—and its important economic role as a major attraction—the Tennessee Aquarium will continue to exhibit the leadership that has already distinguished it as a major force in Chattanooga's renaissance.

RICHARD T. BRYANT

CLOCKWISE FROM TOP:
IN THE AMAZON RIVER FLOODED FOREST EXHIBIT, AQUARIUM EDUCATOR BILL HALEY INTRODUCES STUDENTS TO A TREE FROG.

VISITORS LEAVE THE TENNESSEE AQUARIUM WITH AN APPRECIATION OF HOW THE NATURAL WORLD IS TIED TOGETHER THROUGH MOVING WATER.

THE 12-STORY, 130,000-SQUARE-FOOT BUILDING IS HOME TO MORE THAN 9,000 ANIMALS, INCLUDING A BELUGA STURGEON.

THE HISTORY OF BREAKTHROUGH IDEAS—THOSE THAT CHANGE THE WAY WE think—is littered with related ideas that were far from successful. For example, before the Wright brothers' pioneering flight at Kitty Hawk, an army of would-be "fliers" glued pigeon feathers to their arms, flapped like crazy, and, with one great leap of faith, jumped off the family barn. Needless to say, the results fell short of the expectations.

What drives otherwise rational people to such folly? The answer is easy: excellent ideas—like flying—that haven't been thoroughly thought out.

That lesson has not been lost on Daniel+Douglas+Norcross (ddN), one of Chattanooga's largest and fastest-growing advertising agencies. One look at the firm's portfolio of recent work proves the point. The creative ideas—many of which have earned the agency and its clients advertising awards for excellence— convey more than clever thinking. They uniformly bear the mark of strategic thinking, of addressing the client's communications needs with a solution that works. More important, perhaps, they show ddN's breadth of expertise and ability to fully integrate its thoughts into total marketing campaigns.

INTEGRATED MARKETING PRODUCES RESULTS

ddN's television and print advertising has been recognized for the strategic thinking underlying its messages. Articulated with an award-winning creative flair, the firm's work has produced outstanding results for clients. "We're a regional company with a number of clients doing business nationally and internationally," says Dan Fell, one of the firm's principals. "To serve our clients well, we have to have the depth of talent to see the big picture, make

sense of it, and translate it into a compelling message that energizes all channels of a client's communications plan. We know from experience that this integrated approach generates far more impact than scattershot marketing."

That kind of broad perspective requires diverse skills and capabilities. For example, Phillips|ddN, the agency's public relations arm, is virtually an agency within an agency, offering an array of services aimed at helping clients better deliver their message. After working with the client and the entire ddN team to develop that message, Phillips|ddN manages media relations, provides media training, plans and manages special events, conducts satellite media tours, offers video news releases, and coordinates all aspects of new product launches.

Similarly, ddN Interactive also serves a wide base of client needs.

When clients turn to ddN Interactive for creative, strategic, and logistical support, the firm works together with them to develop a comprehensive Internet, intranet, and extranet strategy that deploys cost-effective TCP/IP-based technologies at points throughout the supply chain, supporting all marketing, operational, and administrative functions. Through this integration of communications and data-handling tools, clients can better serve customers and introduce new efficiencies within its own operation.

Such complexity of client need underscores the importance of fresh ideas to support the evolving nature of communications, not to mention thorough thinking.

CLOCKWISE FROM TOP: (FROM LEFT) DANIEL+DOUGLAS+ NORCROSS (DDN) PARTNERS DAN FELL, ELLEN JOHNSON COOK, AND DOUGLAS COOK UNDERSTAND AND UTILIZE THE POWER OF STRATEGIC THINKING.

ARTICULATED WITH AN AWARD-WINNING CREATIVE FLAIR, THE FIRM'S WORK HAS PRODUCED OUTSTANDING RESULTS FOR CLIENTS.

DDN'S TELEVISION AND PRINT ADVERTISING HAS BEEN RECOGNIZED FOR THE STRATEGIC THINKING UNDERLYING ITS MESSAGES.

DDN IS LOCATED IN HISTORIC DOWNTOWN CHATTANOOGA, IN THE HEART OF NEWLY RENOVATED JACK'S ALLEY.

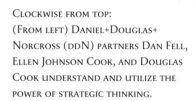

AmSouth Bancorporation

THOUGH A SERIES OF MERGERS BROUGHT AmSOUTH BANK TO Chattanooga in 1993, this relative newcomer has already established itself as one of the area's most visible institutions and a valuable member of the community. The bank has achieved its high profile by delivering on its promise to be the "relationship people," a promise it keeps through the personalized products and services it offers and the civic involvement it actively supports.

Chattanooga is the headquarters city of the Tennessee/Georgia Banking Group of AmSouth Bancorporation, a $20 billion regional holding company based in Birmingham, Alabama. Ranked among the top 50 banking institutions in the United States, AmSouth maintains 275 convenient branch offices and more than 600 ATM installations in Tennessee, Georgia, Alabama, and Florida.

THE PERSONAL TOUCH

Throughout its four-state region, AmSouth is a people-friendly bank that looks to establish strong relationships with customers. According to DeVan D. Ard Jr., president of the Tennessee/Georgia Banking Group, "We want customers to feel good about coming into our banking offices. We believe the way to foster that kind of feeling is through solid relationships. That's why, when customers walk through our doors, they find more than just excellent banking products; they find people committed to providing the kind of personal service that encourages customers to get to know us on a friendly, first-name basis."

AmSouth backs its commitment to personalize the banking experience with extensive, ongoing customer service training for tellers and other branch associates that makes them familiar with the bank's products and services, in order to better serve the customers' needs.

But building strong customer relations takes more than responsive employees. AmSouth also offers products and services that fully meet today's banking needs, from commercial and consumer banking to trust services, private banking, small-business banking, and commercial and residential real estate lending. AmSouth offers customers convenient banking with a toll-free number that is available 24 hours a day, 365 days a year. Customers can also use their personal computers to complete transactions from home, and through telephone banking can pay their bills.

COMMUNITY INVOLVEMENT

AmSouth also has a strong commitment to the Chattanooga community. "We support many worthwhile organizations through sponsorships and contributions, and by encouraging volunteerism among our associates," Ard says.

The bank provides financial support to Allied Arts of Chattanooga, Boy Scouts of America, Tennessee Aquarium, YMCA, Westside Community Development Corporation, and Small Business Development Center.

AmSouth employees play an active role in the community, as well, volunteering in such organizations as Junior Achievement, March of Dimes, United Way, Habitat for Humanity, and Corporate Neighbors Program.

For AmSouth and its employees, relationship banking is more than a marketing slogan. It's a way of life that is having a positive impact on the Chattanooga community.

AmSOUTH IS A PEOPLE-FRIENDLY BANK THAT LOOKS TO ESTABLISH STRONG RELATIONSHIPS WITH CUSTOMERS.

LOUIS SOHN

O PENED IN 1995 BY PRESERVATIONISTS DAVID AND WENDY ADAMS, THE Adams Hilborne Mansion Inn & Restaurant retains all its historic majesty in a grand way that creates a luxurious experience for its guests. This Victorian Romanesque home, built as the mayor's mansion in 1889, faithfully preserves the charm and opulent comfort of that era. ✳ Set in Chattanooga's historic Fort Wood district, the

Adams Hilborne Mansion is of castle-like proportions, featuring 16-foot ceilings, hand-carved moldings, stained-glass windows, native mountain stone, and a stunning array of antiques and period furnishings. The overall effect is of stepping into a more elegant time, when fine architectural detailing was an art, dining was an event, and there was nothing day to day about day-to-day living.

"This home is one of the great treasures of Chattanooga," says owner Wendy Adams, who, with her husband, directed the preservation of the historic mansion. "We've worked carefully to try to retain everything that is original to the home and, in doing so, preserve its natural comfort, grace, and beauty."

Their efforts have not gone unnoticed. The Adams Hilborne Mansion Inn received the prestigious Great American Home Award for 1997 from the National Trust for Historic Preservation. The award, which was bestowed for the Adams' "very sensitive preservation," was one of only three given in the country each year.

TEN UNIQUE GUEST ROOMS

Though restored with all the modern amenities—a renovated, private bath; telephone; fax machine; modem port; television; and VCR—each of the 10 guest rooms is uniquely appointed.

"While we're a boutique hotel offering all the services of a larger hotel," says Adams, "we have preserved our guest rooms, sitting areas, and dining rooms to honor their original design, and thereby, offer our guests a comfortable and

relaxing environment. We like to think of ourselves as an embassy for hospitality."

Overnight guests can choose a room to suit their mood. From the Lookout Suite with its private balcony and spacious sitting area, to the more intimate Chateau Room with its cozy love seat and antique footed tub, the visitor can find a setting appropriate to the moment. No matter what room they select, guests snuggle into cotton sheets under fluffy comforters and rest their heads on piles of downy pillows.

Adams Hilborne dining is as memorable as the inn itself. "My husband and I are travelers," Adams says, "and we like to know there's a great meal awaiting us when we arrive. We want our guests to feel the same way about our inn, so we take special care to offer a menu that will satisfy even the most refined palate."

With elegant dining, a remarkable setting, and an inescapable charm, the memory of a stay at the Adams Hilborne Mansion Inn & Restaurant promises to remain with its guests long after they leave the inn.

CLOCKWISE FROM TOP:

OPENED IN 1995 BY PRESERVATIONISTS DAVID AND WENDY ADAMS, THE ADAMS HILBORNE MANSION INN & RESTAURANT RETAINS ALL ITS HISTORIC MAJESTY IN A GRAND WAY THAT CREATES A LUXURIOUS EXPERIENCE FOR ITS GUESTS.

SET IN CHATTANOOGA'S HISTORIC FORT WOOD DISTRICT, THE ADAMS HILBORNE MANSION IS OF CASTLELIKE PROPORTIONS, FEATURING 16-FOOT CEILINGS, HAND-CARVED MOLDINGS, STAINED-GLASS WINDOWS, NATIVE MOUNTAIN STONE, AND A STUNNING ARRAY OF ANTIQUES AND PERIOD FURNISHINGS.

THE GRACIOUS ENTRANCE TO THE ADAMS HILBORNE MANSION INN WELCOMES GUESTS TO A TRULY MEMORABLE EXPERIENCE.

NOT TOO LONG AGO THE IDEA OF SHREDDING DOCUMENTS CALLED FORTH images of spies disposing of top secret files or gleanings from the latest political cover-up. But in today's business, medical, and legal environment, everyone from the largest multinational corporation to the local bookkeeper accumulates sensitive documents that need timely attention. ✳ Docu-Shred has the solution. Established in Chattanooga in 1995, the firm's specially equipped trucks are driven to a client's location and perform shredding services on-site. Docu-Shred provides businesses with the combination of secure, on-site shredding and the efficiency of a powerful industrial shredder.

Docu-Shred's clients range from the one-man CPA firm to the largest corporations in the area, including hospitals, banks, insurance companies, manufacturing, and even the post office and IRS. While some clients require continuous service, smaller businesses sometimes find using the Docu-Shred service just quarterly or even once a year works adequately for them. For companies of all sizes, having the trucks come on-site offers a no-hassle approach to document disposal.

THE RIGHT IDEA

Many businesses have found that their own shredders break at the most inopportune moments. Additionally, the task of shredding on an undersized machine presents users with problems ranging from broken machines, lost employee productivity, employee injury, and a host of other hassles no one needs. Whatever the case, sensitive documents end up spending too much time in an unsecure environment before being destroyed.

Docu-Shred offers two types of on-site service. A company can simply call and arrange for one of the shredding trucks to come to the property whenever the need arises. Clients can remain with the documents from the time the truck arrives until the time the load is destroyed. In fact, many clients choose to witness the destruction of their documents. Another convenient way to control sensitive information is to have Docu-Shred provide containers in convenient areas of a client's company. These locked, one-way containers are delivered at no charge from Docu-Shred. When needed, a service call can usually be arranged within 24 hours and the containers will be emptied on-site and readied for temporary storage again.

Docu-Shred's industrial shredders can crosscut more than half a ton of material an hour, including staples, paper clips, and even three-ring binders. There is no need to sort out metal pieces, which other shredding machines often require. Furthermore, Docu-Shred's bonded and insured operators guarantee that everything from that particular load gets shredded and, after each session, clients receive a certificate of destruction from the operator. In addition, Docu-Shred cares for the environment by delivering waste material from clients to a recycling plant to cut down on landfill space. "We recycle almost 99.9 percent of the paper material we receive," says Sam Bicking, owner of Docu-Shred.

The whole process is aimed at making document disposal an easy and efficient task. Chattanooga businesses have certainly warmed to the idea—the area client base continues to expand at a promising rate. "We are committed to providing our clients with the highest level of document security possible," says Bicking. "Currently we believe that on-site shredding provides that, and we are always looking for ways to improve upon the best."

A COMPANY CAN SIMPLY CALL AND ARRANGE FOR ONE OF DOCU-SHRED'S TRUCKS TO COME TO THE PROPERTY WHENEVER THE NEED FOR SHREDDING ARISES. CLIENTS CAN REMAIN WITH THE DOCUMENTS FROM THE TIME THE TRUCK ARRIVES UNTIL THE TIME THE LOAD IS DESTROYED.

SINCE COMING TO CHATTANOOGA IN 1996, e.spire HAS OFFERED BUSINESSES powerful voice and data communication services that are integrated through a single sales and support organization, and backed by service commitments. Offering companies powerful "to the point communications," e.spire can consolidate local, long-distance, toll-free, calling card, and audio-conferencing services; provide a single point of

contact for metropolitan and wide-area connectivity, extranet/Internet/intranet support, and managed network services; and offer great prices and service for any of those communications components individually.

ONE-STOP, NONSTOP SERVICE

The company's infrastructure produces high-energy customer care that is supported by proactive account teams; highly skilled engineers; network management 24 hours a day, seven days a week; priority-based problem-resolution processes; and consolidated statements. Local account teams are dedicated to each customer's success. Whether clients require straightforward service connections; optional enhancements; or extensive up-front planning, design, implementation, and management services, e.spire helps determine the scope of the customer's system needs and then implements the total communications package.

The e.spire program manager coordinates all aspects of a client's implementation, including e.spire's resources, the customer's resources, and those of outside suppliers. The e.spire program manager oversees the entire process to ensure a successful installation.

When customers' systems are up and running, e.spire makes sure they stay that way. The company delivers high-quality, reliable, and responsive service 24 hours a day, seven days a week. Additionally, e.spire proactively manages and monitors the client's communications network and system, resulting in an extremely high level of reliability. And since every service request is assigned a priority level based on severity—and is closely tracked through resolution—e.spire operates with the same sense of urgency its customers have.

COMMUNICATIONS SERVICES

The company offers a full array of voice and data communications services. With e.spire, clients can customize voice services with time-saving conveniences designed for mobility and accessibility. They can select from a wide range of productivity options, such as three-way calling, speed dialing, call forwarding, call waiting, and caller ID. They can put voice mail services to work as a personalized answering service. And they can conduct scheduled and impromptu meetings with e.spire audio-conference services.

e.spire also delivers high-speed connectivity options via its metropolitan fiber-optic networks, coast-to-coast data networks, and a full range of high-speed, burstable, and dedicated data services.

The company also offers a full suite of subscription services designed to put the World Wide Web to work for its customers. These services range from high-bandwidth connections to full-service access, Web hosting, newsfeeds, systems monitoring, and support—all with a single point of contact.

e.spire's managed network services make it easy for businesses to be interconnected and Internet-enabled, locally, regionally, nationally, or globally. Several options are available to support varying business needs. They can be optimally configured to complement in-house expertise, or delivered as complete, single-point-of-contact, turnkey solutions.

Led by pioneers in the telecommunications industry, e.spire has rapidly expanded, having established a local presence in many important business markets. It continues to lead the way in building a new breed of integrated communication providers.

E.SPIRE'S STATE-OF-THE-ART NETWORK MANAGEMENT CENTER PROVIDES PRO-ACTIVE 24-HOUR MONITORING OF ALL E.SPIRE SONET NETWORKS, ENSURING HIGH QUALITY AND RELIABILITY.

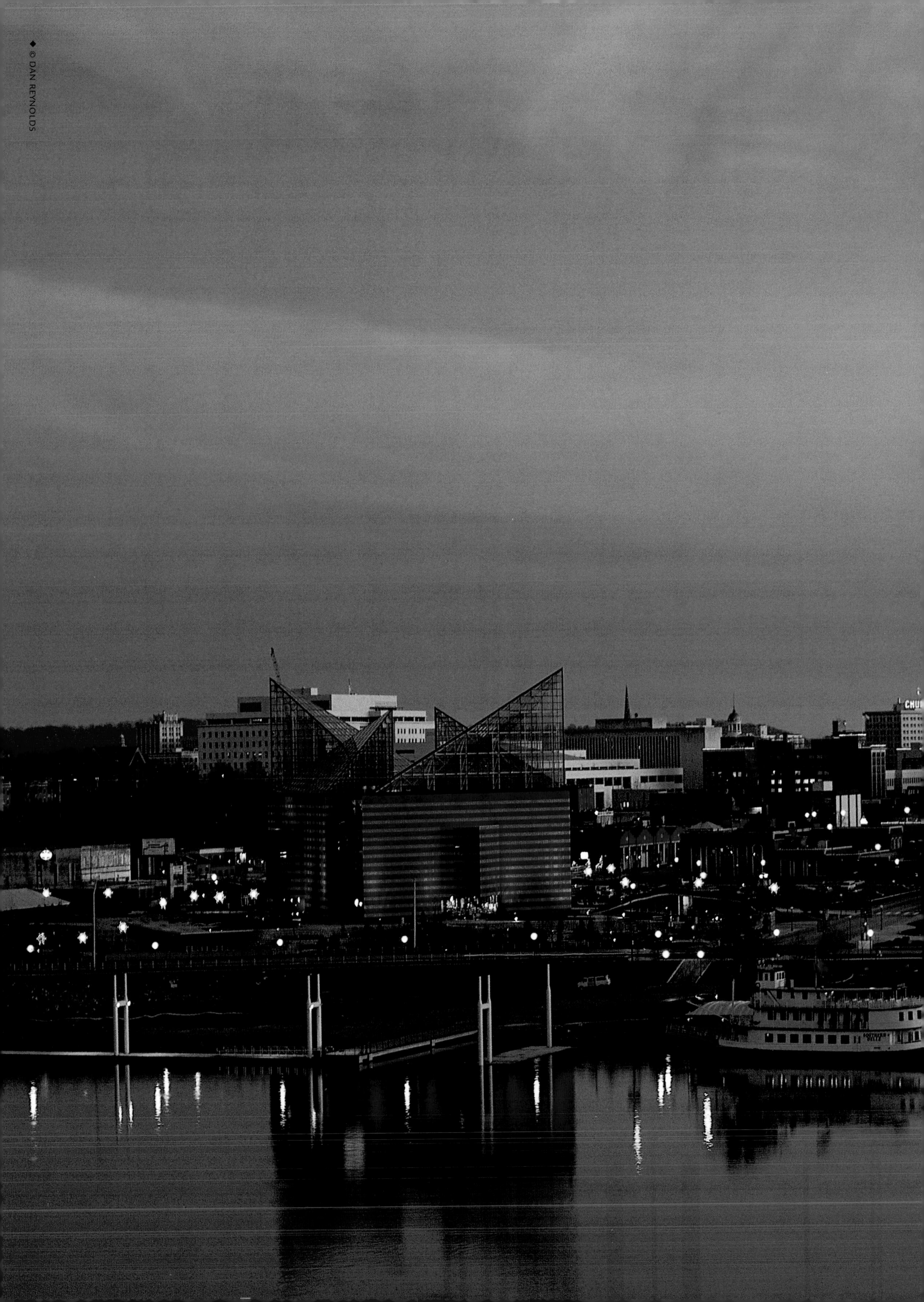

◆ © DAN REYNOLDS

ACKNOWLEDGEMENTS

It was in Washington, D.C., about a decade ago, while I was sitting, stalled, in a taxi at the intersection of Independence and 14th streets, that I knew I wanted to move to Chattanooga. Just like that. Well, sort of.

At the instant the light turned green, we were greeted by a chorus of horns, everyone honking, everyone hurrying. The driver turned and joked, "At least it's better here than in New York. Up there, they start honking even *before* the light changes."

"Down South, where I grew up," I replied, "if you're still sitting at the traffic light when it turns green, someone walks up to your car window and says, 'Ma'am, is there anything I can do to help you?' Back home we only use car horns in town to beep at friends we know so they'll wave back at us." It may have been a bit of an exaggeration, but it's mainly true, and it helps define what I was, at that frantic moment in Washington, missing most about the South: courtesy.

All of this happened just after Desert Storm, as my husband, Lieutenant General Don Rodgers, was making plans to retire from the army. We knew we could move anywhere in America that had an airport because my work with the Challenger Center took me all across the United States, as did visiting our eight grandchildren.

So we sat down to choose a place to call home. To help us decide, my husband—an engineer through and through—created a chart to compare several of our favorite cities and their desirable characteristics. We were both delighted to see that the city of Chattanooga—long one of our favorites—tallied up the most points. We had always loved the combination of river and mountains, both reaching right up to the city's front door, but we had not been fully aware of just how much Chattanooga had to offer until we laid it all out in a kind of grand chart, and made our choice.

Before we knew it, we were on a plane to the city, renting a car, and checking into our room at the historic Read House Hotel. As we walked the tree-lined streets of Broad and Market, we knew our choice was solid, and that we had found a home for the rest of our lives. Eventually, our adult children bought property here, found careers in the area, and moved to Chattanooga to join us with their own families.

So, first off, I need to thank that Washington taxi driver—whoever and wherever he is—for unwittingly and inadvertently reminding me of my love for the South, particularly Chattanooga.

I also want to thank Towery Publishing for asking me to write this narrative about Chattanooga and its renaissance, because it encouraged me to learn even more about my chosen home, its history, its people, and the community that spills into distant valleys and soars across mountains.

Feeling a bit overwhelmed about how to begin the task, I called on my friend Lin Parker at the *Chattanooga Free Press*. She encouraged me to begin with the river, and suggested people who could help. Jim Kennedy, president of the Chattanooga Area Chamber of Commerce and former president of our Convention and Visitors Bureau, was named. Another suggested contact was his predecessor as chamber president, Jim Vaughan. These two sources proved to be invaluable in compiling the research for my introduction to this book.

To try to name all of the others who helped would be futile; so many helped in so many ways that I'm sure to leave out some of the important sources. However, it's important to try to express my thanks to those whose contributions are foremost in my mind: Dave Crockett, Mai Bell Hurley, Jim Bowen, John Franklin, Vilma Fields, Jay Mills, Bill Sudderth, Stroud Watson, Leigh Ferguson, Charlie Arant, Elsa and Jimmie Dotson, Dr. C.C. Bond, Bill Holmberg, Helen Exum, Marcie Pregulman, Rich Bailey, Doug Dougerty, Jack Murrah, John Popham, Norman Burns, Fran and Mitch Simmons, Elizabeth Hare, Bill Owensby, Marty Robinson, Polly Henry, Carole O'Neal, M.K. Bowen, Ann Schimpf, Angela Becksvoort, Priscilla Caine, Lee Johnson, Bob Crawford, Bud Ellis, Mickey Robins, Billy Weeks, Kim Greenwood, Bill Chapin, Judy Kimbro, Dick Kopper, and John Guerry.

I also wish to recognize the valued resources of certain groups, foundations, and organizations, including the Chattanooga Regional History Museum, the Chattanooga Resource Foundation, the Chattanooga News Bureau, River Valley Partners, the Chattanooga-Hamilton County Bicentennial Library, and the city and county offices under the former leadership of Gene Roberts and Dalton Roberts, as well as the current elected officials Jon Kinsey and Claude Ramsey.

In addition, I need to thank family and friends who provided tender words of support: my husband, Don, who helped locate our new home in Chattanooga, and who has encouraged all my efforts in writing this book; my daughter Kathie Fulgham, who shared her expert editing experience; my son Rich Scobee, for his untiring technical support; and my trusted friend Rae Bond, who provided a host of new insights. They all gave me helpful hints that helped shape the narrative. Also, thanks to David Dawson at Towery Publishing and other editors on the company's staff who helped to fashion and polish my narrative.

This book makes no effort to be comprehensive. It is, instead, my impressions of my hometown. Please pardon any inadvertent omissions or missing details, for it is in the details that Chattanooga's charm reveals itself, and it is the details that make it such a beloved place. For those who are already devoted to Chattanooga, may this book serve to fuel that devotion, and to new citizens and visitors alike, may I—like the Washington cab driver I encountered several years ago—help spark interest in Chattanooga.

June Scobee Rodgers

Doug Barnette recently returned to the United States from a tour of Europe where he photographed races and motorcycle events. A resident of Miami, Barnette has received a Gold Medallion Book Award from the Evangelical Christian Publishing Association, Gold Medallion awards for marketing and public relations, Print Industry of America (PIA) awards, and Addy awards.

Edward L. Bowen is employed by the City of Chattanooga in the Department of Public Works-Engineering Division. He enjoys hiking and photographing in the Great Smoky Mountains and has received numerous awards for his work at festivals and shows across Tennessee and Alabama. A dedicated photographer, he even carried a camera on parachute jumps while in the U.S. Army.

Robert C. Boyer and his studio, Shoot the Works, specialize in commercial and architectural photography. His client list includes ABB Combustion Engineering, Provident Companies Inc., Brach & Brock Confections, the Tennessee Valley Authority, Scientific-Atlanta, and Ross/Fowler Architects. A resident of the Chattanooga area since 1965, Boyer won gold Addy awards in 1992 and 1995.

Thomas Cory and his wife, Pat, operate Cory Nature Photography in Signal Mountain. The two have been involved with Sierra Club and Landmark calendars, and have taught workshops throughout the United States since 1974.

Janis L. Dintsch is employed by the Tennessee Valley Authority as a power supply engineer. A member of the Association of Visual Artists

and the Photographic Society of Chattanooga, she is a *Chattanooga Free Press* contest winner. Dintz specializes in travel images and the majority of her clients are private collectors.

Mark Gilliland received an associate of science degree in photography from Daytona Beach Community College in Florida. The lab manager at a one-hour photo lab, Gilliland uses his spare time to photograph landscapes and abstract designs. His images have been distributed by United Press International and the Associated Press, and have appeared in *Country Weekly* magazine.

David M. Grant graduated from Tennessee Technological University with a bachelor of science degree in biology. Born and raised in Chattanooga, Grant is employed by Grant, Konvalinka & Harrison, P.C. as a legal assistant. His work was featured on the Agfa Photography Web site as Photograph of the Month for August 1997.

Stephen Greenfield is a nationally published, self-taught photographer from Nashville whose areas of specialty include advertising, corporate, and editorial images. A former police detective and a resident of Cleveland, Tennessee, he has been a professional photographer for 33 years.

Jeff Guenther lives in Signal Mountain with his wife and two children. Employed by the *Chattanooga Times* for 15 years, Guenther has been published in *Newsweek, Time,* and *USA Today.* He has received awards from the National Press Photographers Association and the Associated Press.

Robert E. Keebler was born in Coalmont, Tennessee, and moved to Chattanooga in 1958. He is a retired school teacher and a former National Park Service ranger. In addition to contributing photographs to various brochures, Keebler has been published in *Southern Living* and *Sky and Telescope.*

Bud Lee studied at the Columbia University School of Fine Arts in New York and the National Academy of Fine Arts before moving to the Plant City, Florida, area more than 20 years ago. A self-employed photojournalist, he founded both the Florida Photographers Workshop and the Iowa Photographers Workshop. Lee's work can be seen in *Esquire, Life, Travel & Leisure, Rolling Stone,* the *Washington Post,* and the *New York Times,* as well as in Towery Publishing's *Treasures on Tampa Bay: Tampa, St. Petersburg, Clearwater; Orlando: The City Beautiful; Jacksonville: Reflections of Excellence;* and *Greater Syracuse: Center of an Empire.*

James Madden recently returned from a year in Russia, where he worked as a photographer for various advertising agencies. Originally from Daytona Beach, Florida, Madden currently resides in Red Bank, Tennessee.

Troy E. Moore Sr. is an avid amateur photographer, shooting some 600 rolls of film a year. Although he focuses on macro, scenic, wildlife, and sports images, his true passion lies in photographing old barns and waterfalls.

Dan Reynolds, owner of Dan Reynolds Photography, lives in Atlanta, but works in Chattanooga one to two days a week. His clients include area advertising agencies,

corporations, and businesses, and his line of Chattanooga postcards is available in many local stores. Reynolds has also won the bronze award in the International Festivals Association competition in Canada.

Edward S. Richards received a bachelor of science degree in building construction from Hampton University in Virginia. A retired Tennessee Valley Authority graphic designer, Richards now devotes his time to freelance photography. Although he specializes in scenic and creative still-life images, Richards has also photographed celebrities visiting the Chattanooga area, most notably Jackie Robinson and Jessie Owens.

Vicki Rozema is the author of *Footsteps of the Cherokees: A Guide to the Eastern Homelands of the Cherokee Nation,* which received a certificate of merit from the Tennessee Historical Commission. Her photographs have been published in *Blue Ridge Country, Country, National Parks, Farm and Ranch Living, Taste of Home, Now and Then,* and *Birds & Blooms* magazines. A former president of the Photographic Society of Chattanooga, she has been a photographer for 23 years.

Robin Rudd, a lifelong resident of Chattanooga, has been employed by the *Chattanooga Free Press* as a staff photographer for 18 years. He received a bachelor's degree from Middle Tennessee State University. Rudd and his wife, Pamela, have five children: Rachel, Maggie, Rebecca, Charles, and Anne.

Scott Turner received an associate's degree in nuclear technology from Chattanooga

State Technical Community College. As owner of Scott Turner Photography, he includes among his clients D.C. McDonald and Associates, Inc., Conoco, and IMAGES Photography. In 1996, Turner won the Members' Choice Award from the Photographic Society of Chattanooga.

Billy Weeks serves as photography editor/team leader at the *Chattanooga Times,* as well as a part-time journalism instructor at Southern College. His images have appeared in a variety of publications, including *U.S News & World Report, USA Today, Travel Week, Trade and Convention,* the *Tennessean, Forbes, People,* and *Time.* Weeks has received awards for his sports action and feature photography from the National Press Photographers Association, the Tennessee Press Association, and the Tennessee Associated Press. He served as the photography editor for Towery's *Chattanooga: Delivering the Dream,* published in 1991.

Gregory Williams, a lifelong resident of Savannah, Georgia, has studied under renowned nature photographer John Earl. Williams specializes in landscape, unique architecture, and abstract photography, and many of his images have appeared in chamber of commerce guides across the nation. The winner of several regional Sierra Club photo contests, he mounted an exhibition titled *Savannah and the Georgia Coast* in 1996. His images have also appeared in Towery Publishing's *Seattle: Pacific Gem.*

Additional photographers and organizations that contributed to *Chattanooga: River City Renaissance* include Ewing Galloway, Inc., Hillstrom Stock Photo, Scott C. Lee, and James E. Myers II.

INDEX OF PROFILES

CHATTANOOGA